Endorsem

Jesus instructed his disciples to remain in him as a
vine. At no point in ones Christian life do they reac
that will allow them to dislocate themselves from th
clarified that apart from him, we can do nothing. Our union with Christ is our life-source, our greatest privilege, and our joy-producing reality. All ministry that would bear lasting fruit must be grounded in this. Dr. Burns, from years of experience serving in missions and ministry, writes with a passion to remind Great Commission-minded people that their source of hope and fruitfulness is not tethered to their enthusiasm, boldness, or novelty. Rather, it is born of vital union with Christ. His book, *Great Commission Spirituality*, serves as a grounding reminder of the privilege that it is to draw our life from the one whose name we intend to proclaim to the ends of the earth. You will walk away grateful for his faithful reminder—and example—of the fact that we are an "in-Christ" people who are graced with the opportunity to make much of the king in every corner of his realm.

Matt Bennett, PhD
Director of Long-Term Ministries,
Reaching and Teaching International Ministries

In commissioning his disciples to takes the good news to the ends of the earth, the risen Lord promised that he would be with them and to give him his Spirit. We should not be surprised then that many of those who have experienced the reality of union with Christ most deeply and written about it most profoundly have been men and women caught up in obeying that commission. Burns has not only imbibed the best of that literature but has added to it. *Great Commission Spirituality* is not a book that readers will finish and set aside. It's a book they will underline and quote, save and share, and return to and savor. I highly recommend it.

Steve Bryan, PhD
Professor of New Testament, Trinity Evangelical Divinity School

It is far too common for us Great Commission servants, both new and experienced, to labor under the crushing weight of not being or doing enough. As a result, we anxiously strive to discover and implement new habits and methods that will unlock greater faith and fruitfulness. So often, those efforts appear spiritual, but in the end, they leave us feeling more discouraged and exhausted. In this book, Burns aims to alleviate this burdened way of living by pointing us to the rest and freedom we have through our union with Christ. By mining the writings of missionary giants who have gone before us, Burns demonstrates how their fruitfulness and joyful service was rooted in the doctrine of the "great exchange." If you have ever felt burdened or ineffective in your labors for the Great Commission, as I have, then this book will be a balm for your soul. As you read it, let it draw you near to Christ, in whom we have everything we need for a life of service that is filled with joy, rest, and genuine fruitfulness.

Matt Deaver, PhD
Professor of Theology and Missions, Malaysia Baptist Theological Seminary

Nourishing. Joyous. Energizing. Strengthening. Amazing. These are some of the words I'd use to describe the experience of reading Burns' *Great Commission Spirituality*. If you know Christ, this book will draw you closer to him. If you're in ministry, this book will cause you to grow strong from Christ's own strength. If you're considering missions, you'll be motivated and instructed. And if you've been making disciples among the unreached for the better part of a century, you'll have your heart drawn closer to where Christ is, seated at the right hand of God. This book will leave you awestruck as you gaze at the glories of the Creator who unites himself to his creatures.

Derek Joseph
Director of Recruitment, Pioneers

Dr. Burns's contribution to Great Commission studies uniquely shows how our union with Christ is our identity and all our ministry flows from there. Many authors have highlighted the importance of "character" in mission and leadership. Yet, this book unpacks the concept of "godly character" in a beautiful way, so as to come from union with Christ. This book is remarkably applicable to all ages and all cultures of the global church.

Emmanuel Kwizera
Catalyst for Proclamation Evangelism, Lausanne Movement
International Missions Director, African Enterprise

In the trenches of Christian life and ministry, we can so easily lose sight of what is central and most needed. Burns has written a wonderfully refreshing reminder to Christians of the precious treasure we possess in union with our Lord Jesus. Being united to Christ by faith fuels and motivates our obedience to his Great Commission. Amid trials, when we suffer discouragement and disappointments in life and ministry, the truth that "Christ is in us and with us and for us in everything" propels us forward with courage and confidence. I highly recommend this encouraging book.

Eugene Low
Lead teaching Pastor, Grace Baptist Church, Singapore

What feeds and forms our Christian service? In *Great Commission Spirituality*, Dr. Burns answers this question by explaining that rest, prayer, meditation, contemplation, witnessing, humility, and courage are not mere rote disciplines of the Christian life, but rather are the product of our union in Christ, which then become the spiritual instincts we use to boldly and joyfully labor as ambassadors for His glory and kingdom. Regardless of your calling, this timely and convicting book will challenge your thinking on why we fulfill the Great Commission while pointing you to the real power that sustains us as we proclaim the good news of Jesus Christ to all peoples.

John A. Tucker
Pastor, Community Bible Church, Beloit, Ohio

Running on empty at the end of the earth? Maybe you thought the glory of the Great Commission would fill you up. But as this book reminds us, that is the glorious work of the Great Commissioner himself—*with you* and *in you*, *for you* and *before you*. Burns lives the encouraging truth that leaps from every page in this book: Christ alone is your home away from home.

Trent Hunter
Pastor for Preaching and Teaching,
Heritage Bible Church, Greer, South Carolina

Burns knows the distinctive spiritual challenges of missionaries from experience and gives us a master class on the heart of a missionary. He both points to the history of missions for paradigms of faithful discipleship and directs us back to who we are in Jesus as the foundation for long-term fruitfulness. Every "Great Commission Ambassador" will find sustenance for an authentic pursuit of excellence in this book.

Jon Hoglund, PhD
Associate Professor of Theology and Global Studies,
Bethlehem College and Seminary

Great Commission Spirituality: Abiding in Christ, Serving in Obscurity

William Carey Publishing (WCP) publishes resources to shape and advance the missiological conversation in the world. We publish a broad range of thought-provoking books and do not necessarily endorse all opinions set forth here or in works referenced within this book.

The URLs included in this workbook are provided for personal use only and are current as of the date of publication, but the publisher disclaims any obligation to update them after publication.

Published by William Carey Publishing
10 W. Dry Creek Cir
Littleton, CO 80120 | www.missionbooks.org

William Carey Publishing is a ministry of Frontier Ventures
Pasadena, CA | www.frontierventures.org

Cover and Interior Designer: Mike Riester

ISBNs: 978-1-64508-570-6 (paperback)
978-1-64508-572-0 (epub)

Printed Worldwide

28 27 26 25 24 1 2 3 4 5 IN

Library of Congress Control Number: 2024938753

GREAT COMMISSION Spirituality

Abiding in Christ, Serving in Obscurity

E. D. Burns

Dedicated to:
Dao

A gift I do not deserve.
A treasure better than I could imagine.

Union to Jesus
is the humble Christian's life,
his hope,
his all.

—W. C. Burns

Contents

Foreword

Spiritual maturity, or flourishing as a Christian servant, is a walk marked by "a long obedience in the same direction," to cite the title of one of Eugene Peterson's books on the nature of Christian discipleship. In other words, mature Christian living is a life's work, a task stretching over years and decades. Of course, this rubs against the grain of modern culture, which expects all that it desires in the here and now and is, in fact, used to instant this and instant that.

This new study, by a veteran missionary, explores the means of grace that comprise "long obedience"—prayer, meditation, and contemplation. This book also discusses the virtues that "long obedience" creates—humility and courage. Indeed, the Christian life takes sweat and toil and tears.

Earlier generations prior to the twentieth century knew this all too well. In a world of significant infant mortality, no antibiotics, and few painkillers, people seem to have been more prepared to face struggle and suffering with dogged perseverance and resourceful courage than we are in the West today. One thinks of the challenges faced by William Carey, for example: the six-month-long voyage to India; the death of his son Peter within a year of their landing that led in part to the complete mental deterioration of his wife Dorothy; the lack of converts for the first seven years of his ministry; then, the great fire at the Serampore Press in March of 1812 that destroyed years of translation labour along with precious paper, fonts, and printing tools; and finally, the rupture between the Serampore Trio and the Baptist Missionary Society in England after the death of Andrew Fuller in 1815. Throughout all of this, Carey and his close co-workers, William Ward and Joshua and Hannah Marshman, remained undeterred in their commitment to the mission in India, and, as Carey once remarked of himself, they plodded on in faith and hope and with grit and gumption.

I have known the author of this book, Dr. E. D. Burns, for fifteen years, a few of which he spent in taking doctoral seminars at my school in biblical spirituality. He wrote a doctoral thesis on the spirituality of Carey's famous contemporary, Adoniram Judson, a remarkable missionary to southeast Asia, whose life story never fails to inspire. Alongside his studies in the history of Christian spirituality, Burns has also participated in the reality of discipleship as a missionary in the cross-cultural context in Southeast Asia.

Thus, in writing this book about the dynamics of the Christian life, Burns draws not only from the reservoir of spiritual riches found in the history of the church, but also from the daily challenges of living out his faith in a Buddhist environment.

And I am honored and pleased to commend this book.

MICHAEL A. G. AZAD HAYKIN
Director, The Andrew Fuller Center for Biblical Studies
Professor, Church History and Biblical Spirituality,
The Southern Baptist Theological Seminary

Dundas, Ontario
April 2024

Preface

As in all my books, I write from my background—an ordained minister; a trained linguist; a seminary professor of historical theology, biblical spirituality, and missiology; and as someone who has served vocationally in missions since the early 2000s. I have served in rural and urban places teaching both children and doctoral students. I have served in pastoral ministry and mercy ministry while studying a handful of unrelated languages and living with my family in the Middle East, East Asia, Southeast Asia, and Alaska. As I tell my seminary students, understanding the background of an author helps one understand the foreground of their writing.

But that is just a bland, obligatory introduction. It does not capture how God has shaped me from affliction, accusation, bereavement, and distress; nor does it encapsulate who I am in person as a professor, missionary, friend, and father. Not to mention who I am as a struggler, a sinner, and an underwhelmingly ordinary man in the service of an extraordinary God. I hope to write honestly and somewhat autobiographically to share the encouragement of the valuable lessons I have learned over the last twenty-five years. I wish I could have just learned these lessons from a book or a class, but that's not how God usually trains us, is it? He grows us imperceptibly in seasons of droughts, downpours, frozen fields, pruning, and sunshine. Trees grow deeply below the surface before they bear fruit above. No seedling grows into a flourishing fruit tree overnight. Trees grow slowly and subtly. The person I am today is not who I was when I started—praise the Lord. And if he gives me twenty-five more years of life in his service, I pray that I will be less like the old me and more like Jesus.

The chapters of this book are intentionally diverse in style—some are more reflective and devotional, while others are more theological and apologetic. A few are more practical and concrete. Some chapters will seem like I am speaking frankly and naturally as though in a casual conversation. Other chapters might seem more like a sermon, and others like a lecture. One reason for the diversity of style is to model that we grow spiritually in relationship with others as we listen to the lives of others, sit under the teaching of others, and receive the blessing of gospel proclamation.

Though I speak candidly on some controversial issues, I hope these chapters will not encourage moralism and legalism but rather faith and hope in the kindness and benevolence of God. More than a taskmaster to smack us around, we need a friend who will not snuff out the smoking flax or break the bruised reed. We all struggle to do our best with the talents, gifts, personalities, health, status, and measure of faith that God has appointed us despite our deep flaws and weakness. We're all unremarkable, simple servants serving a remarkable, sovereign God.

In the end, I felt the need to cut out a handful of chapter ideas for the sake of length and accessibility. The most difficult part of writing a book is choosing what not to say. I've left out many topics that would have been beneficial, yet I trust that this book will deeply encourage the hearts of men and women in the Lord's service around the world, who are actively seeking to obey the Great Commission.

This book is not exclusively for traditional missionaries. Any gospel servant in any country can benefit from the useful principles included here. I want to especially encourage Great Commission ambassadors who feel like the Great Commission comes at too great a cost. The promised blessings can seem like mirages in a desert—fading and never fully satisfying. This book is for the languishing servant who needs an encouraging word, helpful insight, and fresh hope that God is always faithful to his servants. "Like cold water to a thirsty soul, so is good news from a far country" (Prov 25:25). I hope this book helps you see the fingerprints of God's subtle providence in your life and your vocation, and in God's world and God's word. To that end, the Great Commission spirituality of this book will underscore evangelical virtues and practical truths that instruct, challenge, and comfort.

Introduction

Serving in Light of God's Promises in Christ

Scripture for Meditation:

You have said, "Seek my face."
My heart says to you,
"Your face, LORD, do I seek."
—Psalm 27:8

A nineteenth-century missionary in China recalled in a letter, "We are all, as I believe, serving God in our divine vocations, with greater gladness, and more fervid zeal, from having communed with your brother in his heavenly walk and noble aspirations." Another missionary retorted, when asked about this man, "Know him, sir? ... All China knows him."[1] Who was this man that influenced missionaries all over China?

W. C. Burns was a famous revivalist from Glasgow. He preached throughout Scotland and Canada. Ahead of him lay a future of ministry renown and influence beyond his peers. Yet, the Lord seemed to burden him instead with a passion for reaching the unreached of China. Instead of fame, his life would be marked by stark simplicity, self-denial, and obscurity. Driven by a heart for the unreached, Burns noted that God's providence eventually led him to refresh the souls of struggling missionaries throughout China. His message to the missionaries? Having Christ and losing this world is the happiest life. He often said,

> The happiest state of a Christian on earth seems to be this—that he should have *few wants*. If a man have Christ in his heart, and heaven before his eye, and only as much of temporal blessings as is just needful to carry him safely through life, then pain and sorrow have little to shoot at—such a man has very little to lose. To be in union with Him, who is the Shepherd of Israel, and to walk very near to Him who is a sun and a shield—that comprehends all that a poor sinner requires to make him happy between this and heaven.[2]

1 Burns, *Memoir of William*, 333. See also Houghton, *Five Pioneer Missionaries*; McMullen, *God's Polished Arrow*; Burns, *Revival Sermons*.

2 Burns, *Memoir of William*, 333. Emphasis in original.

Burns had tasted the fruit of evangelical renewal in Scotland ministering alongside Robert Murray M'Cheyne in 1839. His evangelistic desire to awaken nominal and cultural Christians from their slumber led him to China. In 1855, Burns met a young Hudson Taylor. While Taylor influenced Burns with his adoption of Chinese dress and customs, Burns became Taylor's spiritual mentor. Taylor recounted Burns's spiritual investment into his life: "Those happy months were an unspeakable joy and privilege to me. His love for the Word was delightful, and his holy, reverential life and constant communings with God made fellowship with him satisfying to the deep cravings of my heart."[3]

Taylor felt captivated by the tender spirit with which Burns drew near to Christ in prayer. That sweet communion with Christ seemed to fill Burns with an uncommonly courageous zeal for the Chinese to hear the word of Christ. The early years Taylor spent ministering with Burns indelibly stamped upon his soul the truth that Great Commission service required an evangelical spirituality. The Great Commission is under Christ's authority (Matt 28:18) and within Christ's abiding presence (Matt 28:20). Those truths are the bedrock of the Great Commission's sure success. Therefore, our fundamental task is to prayerfully rest in these promises and boldly labor in the power of our union with Christ.

Main Take-Aways

This book aims to encourage and instruct Great Commission servants to (1) endure by faith in God's promises; (2) abide in Christ; (3) live in hope of Christ's now-and-not-yet kingdom; and (4) testify boldly to the honor of the King. This assumes that our Great Commission service should be word-driven and Christ-centered.[4]

Great Commission service is only as long-lasting and fruitful as the spirituality that fuels it. And that spirituality is only as good as its theology. For those who are inheritors of the blessings of the Protestant Reformation, the Great Commission servant should at least hold to the five *solas* of the Protestant Reformation as a theological grid for their

3 Taylor, *Hudson Taylor Collection*, 7, Kindle Edition, Location 783.

4 For a more developed ideas on what this means theologically and looks like practically, see Burns, *Missionary-Theologian*. I use the common evangelical "Christ-centered" terminology, though I prefer a hermeneutic called the "Christotelic" approach. I discuss this in Burns, *Ancient Gospel*, 40–64.

spirituality and service: salvation is for the glory of God alone, according to Scripture alone, by grace alone, through faith alone, in Christ alone. "Great Commission spirituality must first emerge from a hearty trust in the triune God, and then it should grow out of and bear fruit from the power of the Word of Christ. It should result in a restful, glad-hearted contentment in God. It therefore labors freely and gratefully to the glory of God and salvation of the nations."[5]

This book weaves the central doctrine of union with Christ through each chapter. And the instinct to prayerfully abide in Christ is the application throughout. Most chapters seek to apply what my PhD supervisor at Southern Baptist Theological Seminary, Michael A.G. Haykin, called *historical spiritual mentorship*. He himself modeled spiritual mentorship for me. Contemplating the flawed life and warm piety of humble saints of the past has been determinative in my approach to this book. Moreover, I have highlighted virtues I have learned from my contemporary mentors who have written their teachings on my soul through spiritual friendship. I cannot mention them all by name, since God has kindly given me so many, but I seek to give credit to most of them at least in the footnotes or the acknowledgements.

Each chapter will devotionally reflect on our union with Christ, how it affects various aspects of our Great Commission spirituality, and the power and privilege of praying in him to the Father for all our Great Commission service. As we remember and rejoice in the promises of our union with Christ, my prayer is that we will increase in Christlike virtue. Such virtue gives way to effective and fruitful Great Commission service (2 Pet 1:3–8). And as we grow in virtue and the sweet knowledge of our union with Christ, may we be watchful of our lives and our doctrine: "Keep a close watch on yourself and on the teaching. Persist in this, for by so doing you will save both yourself and your hearers" (1 Tim 4:16). As we stand like sentinels over our virtue and the doctrine we teach, God will bless us and our hearers with the fruit of salvation.

I pray that the theological applications of this book would give us strength to contend for the supremacy and sufficiency of Christ's word (as our Prophet), to endure with a glad-hearted contentment in Christ's

5 Burns, *Seeds and Stars*, 3. Moreover, I describe (not define) the general process of holy living in Burns, *Seeds and Stars*, 6.

sovereign authority (as our King), and to enjoy the sweet fellowship of our union with Christ (as our Priest) in the inglorious obscurity of Great Commission service. May we "be steadfast, immovable, always abounding in the work of the Lord, knowing that in the Lord your labor is not in vain" (1 Cor 15:58).

A Prayerful Instinct that Plods on in Love for Christ

This book seeks to encourage a prayerful *instinct* of the heart, a communion with God. By instinct, I mean that inclination or fondness that comes from our new nature in Christ—not the old nature in Adam. Not all my points are actionable items. The virtues that we develop as Christians are on a spectrum between mindsets and practices. I will touch on some practices, but I focus mostly on the mindset and affection of faith—knowledge, assent, and hearty trust in the promises of God in Christ.

If one chapter of Scripture could show how our union with Christ should affect our Great Commission spirituality and service, it would be Colossians 1. In fact, I encourage you to prayerfully read the book of Colossians as you read this book. Many themes from Colossians guide the aims of this book. May portions like these verses influence you as you reflect on the truths of this book:

> To them God chose to make known how great among the Gentiles are the riches of the glory of this mystery, which is Christ in you, the hope of glory. Him we proclaim, warning everyone and teaching everyone with all wisdom, that we may present everyone mature in Christ. For this I toil, struggling with all his energy that he powerfully works within me. (Col 1:27–29)

Let the light of our union with Christ shine through the windows of God's word and God's world to revive our souls. He has united us to his beloved Son in love, to pour out upon us deluge after deluge of lavish kindness, age after age for all eternity. Now, with the strength he supplies, let us go serve him another mundane day, plodding on with a hopeful contentment. For the love of Christ controls us.

> *Christ is the desire of nations, the joy of angels, the delight of the Father. What solace then must that soul be filled with, that has the possession of Him to all eternity!*
>
> —John Bunyan

Chapter 1

Rest

Abiding in Christ and the Peace of God

Scripture for Meditation:

> According to the riches of his glory he may grant you to be strengthened with power through his Spirit in your inner being, so that Christ may dwell in your hearts through faith—that you, being rooted and grounded in love, may have strength to comprehend with all the saints what is the breadth and length and height and depth, and to know the love of Christ that surpasses knowledge, that you may be filled with all the fullness of God.
>
> —Ephesians 3:16–19

Fifteen years after serving in missions, I could finally take a break. And no, I don't mean a vacation or holiday. True, I had just finished my PhD, and my wife was severely ill. But what I needed more than a break from the chaos of my external circumstances was a break from my own expectations and the expectations others had of me.

Some of my supervisors and leaders in the mission field exuded a victorious life. They recalled how things went spectacularly well for those who learned to listen to God's still voice and act upon it with unflinching obedience. The strong implication was that if we, also, listened to the

Spirit's guidance and acted on it by faith, we too would have good success. We would live to tell tales of God's special anointing and blessing.

To be fair, they probably did not mean to communicate it all this way. They are works-in-progress just as I am. And while I probably misinterpreted their advice at times, sometimes, it was word-for-word, just as I relayed it above. These expectations led me to years of simmering anxiety and frustration with myself for not working hard enough, studying the language enough, practicing their disciple-making movement methods enough, or praying sincerely enough. Yet, God slowly began to open my eyes to see his work differently. Adoniram Judson, Andrew Fuller, Hudson Taylor, Martin Luther, Augustine, Thomas Boston, and others, were my teachers. They showed me how to work with all my might. But at the same time, they showed me how to rest in Christ. John G. Paton, missionary to the New Hebrides, described it this way:

> I pity from the depth of my heart every human being, who, from whatever cause, is a stranger to the most ennobling, uplifting, and consoling experience that can come to the soul of man—blessed communion with the Father of our Spirits, through gracious union with the Lord Jesus Christ. … "Come unto Me, all ye that labour and are heavy laden, and I will give you rest. Take My yoke upon you, and learn of Me; for I am meek and lowly in heart: and ye shall find rest unto your souls. For My yoke is easy, and My burden is light."[1]

Whether I achieved much, little, or nothing, and even if I lost everything, Christ vowed to be with me for the honor of his name. He pledged to be my Friend through it all. But more than that, sweet as it is, Christ is my life. I am his. Our union is unbreakable. Nothing and no one can sever me from God's love in Christ. What God has joined together, let no man rend asunder. God hates divorce. That covenantal security in Christ gave me the courage to stay the course.

Hudson Taylor and Strength in Christ

As the end of each year approaches in December, I, like most Great Commission servants, hold deep regrets and disappointments. Before my mind are all my failures: the lack of fruitfulness in ministry, inadequacy as

1 Paton, *John G. Paton*, Kindle Edition, Location 6430.

a godly father, insufficiency in language learning, and all the other spiritual and natural habits and goals that I fall short of keeping well enough. It's in this context that the joyful discovery of a justified life in Christ has given me (like so many others in church history) the courage to plod on.

The great missionary to the interior of China, Hudson Taylor, received a letter from a dear friend during a painfully dark season on the mission field. The letter commended the doctrine of union with Christ, which Taylor had heard before from Keswick influences in his earlier years.

This was not a new theological system for Taylor. But, as God is so kind to his servants, he opened Taylor's eyes to see into a fresh window of the heavenly reality of life in Christ. Joy in Christ was what turned a black and white vision of that doctrine into living color. And Taylor would heartily confirm, "oh, how joy flowed!"[2]

Taylor was not a naïve "let-go-and-let-God" Pietist. As a hard-working laborer in his Lord's vineyard, he believed in spending himself for evangelism and spiritual growth. He pioneered past the civilized and colonized coastlands of China. And he endeavored past the advice of his more realistic superiors. His sold-out venture into the vast, troubled interior demonstrates that he had no lazy, passive bone in his body. His spiritual nerve was steely, probably to a fault. He implied that his burned-out state as a Great Commission servant led him to the blessed truth of "the exchanged life."

It is a shame that so many Great Commission servants don't ever read Taylor and yet automatically lump him together with theologically unmoored Keswick mystics. I was one of those, until I read Taylor's spiritual autobiography for myself. I'm no Taylor scholar—I haven't read his life and works exhaustively like I have others. So there could be some pieces I might hesitate to recommend. But that's how we all are—none of us gets it all right, all the time, all our lives. Yet, what I have read in Taylor's spiritual autobiography has been truly refreshing.

Taylor displayed a stubborn devotion to God's uncommon assignments, while possessing an abiding assurance in his union with Christ. His Christ-centered restfulness galvanized his Great Commission resilience. In his foreword to Taylor's book, *Union and Communion*, J. Stuart Holden cautioned against the knee-jerk reaction to dismiss Taylor as an impractical mystic:

2 Taylor, *Hudson Taylor's Spiritual Secret*, 84.

> It is inevitable that there are those who will read and reject as mystical and unpractical, that which is so directly concerned with the intimacies of fellowship with the unseen Lord. I would, however, venture to remind such that the writer of these pages founded the China Inland Mission! He translated his vision of the Beloved into life-long strenuous service.[3]

In other words, Taylor was not an idle quietist. He was no dogmatist of Keswick theology. Taylor's discovery of life in Christ differed from other Keswick contemporaries. This is a valuable lesson for how God can use bits of truth amidst the excesses of a theologically faulty movement to steer his servants to Christlikeness. He chewed the meat and spit out the bones, as it were. God used imperfectly worded Keswick sentiments to mercifully deliver Taylor from an exhausting, never-good-enough frenetic spirit.

Six months before Taylor discovered the "blessed reality [that] 'Christ liveth in me,'" he wrote this: "I have continually to mourn that I follow at such a distance and learn so slowly to imitate my precious Master."[4] But once the Lord opened Taylor's eyes to see into his union with Christ, his perspective of everything changed indelibly: "There was no thought of imitation now! … And how great the difference!—instead of bondage, liberty; instead of failure, quiet victories within; instead of fear and weakness, a restful sense of sufficiency in Another."[5]

He said, "I prayed, agonised, fasted, strove, made resolutions, read the Word more diligently, sought more time for meditation—but all without avail. … I knew that if only I could abide in Christ all would be well, but I could not. … To will was indeed 'present with me,' but how to perform I found not."[6] He would go on to admit that he intellectually knew that Christ was all he needed. He intellectually knew only abiding in him as a branch in the vine was necessary. But how was he to access that true life? He knew it was through faith: "I strove for faith, but it would not come; I tried to exercise it, but in vain. … I prayed for faith, but it came not. What was I to do?"[7] In other words, he was putting his faith in his perceived quality of faith, not in Christ.

---

3 Holden, "Foreword," Kindle Edition, Location 1973.

4 Taylor, *Hudson Taylor's Spiritual Secret*, 86.

5 Taylor, 86.

6 Taylor, 86.

7 Taylor, 86.

Taylor's discovery of this exchanged life—bondage for freedom, fear for peace—was found in a small word. That overlooked word distinguished the Protestant Reformation from the works-infused systems of Roman Catholicism and medieval mysticism. Both systems attempted to mix and conflate God's assisting grace with our efforts. What was the goal? To attain a justified life of union with Christ. Did they affirm grace? Yes. Did they promote faith? Yes. So, what was that small word that made all the difference between life within Christ and life without Christ? *Sola*. Alone. Salvation by grace alone, through faith alone, in Christ alone, according to Scripture alone, to the glory of God alone. Of those five *solas*, which is the instrument that receives Christ and all his benefits? *Sola fide*. Faith alone.

Taylor was already a devout Great Commission servant, pouring himself out for the good of China and the glory of God. Yet, for the first time, Taylor discovered the great exchange: Christ's righteous life imputed to sinners through faith alone and our sin's penalty imputed to him on the cross. Before understanding this foundational truth, Taylor sought assurance through a mixture of his faith in Christ with his Great Commission faithfulness and holy habits. Taylor recalled that glorious sentence from his friend's letter mentioned above. Here is how faith alone in Christ alone fortified his assurance and arrested his attention:

> "But how to get faith strengthened? Not by striving after faith, but by resting on the Faithful One." As I read, I saw it all! "If we believe not, he abideth faithful." I looked to Jesus and saw (and when I saw, oh, how joy flowed!) that He had said, "I will never leave thee." "Ah, *there* is rest!" I thought. "I have striven in vain to rest in Him. I'll strive no more. For has not *He* promised to abide with me—never to leave *me*, never to fail me?" And, dearie, *He never will*.[8]

Taylor's spiritual mentor in China, W. C. Burns, put it like this:

> The believer, who has begun to learn the value of Christ, does not find difficulty in determining whether to give up one thing, or two things, or many things for Christ, and whether he should still be repaid for so doing. He is not always hesitating and calculating whether Christ will make this or that loss to him. He has Christ, thrice blessed portion, and in Him, all. He would not seek earthly

8 Taylor, 87. Emphasis in the original.

> riches or honours, even if he could get them. All he has, all he is, is already Christ's—by purchase—by free surrender—and by wonderful, glorious exchange. All that Christ has is his too, he is a joint-heir with Christ. He gets all *from* heaven, returns all to heaven, and the heart that is already at home there, has not much time for earthly pleasure.[9]

Taylor discovered that faith alone is the weak hand that reaches out and is secured by the strong arm of Christ. This is the justified life of resting united with Christ through faith alone. There is a stillness of soul for those who have discovered this treasure. Some, like Martin Luther, William Tyndale, John Bunyan, and John Wesley, discovered the joy of this great exchange in the doctrine of Christ's imputed righteousness; others, like Hudson Taylor, W. C. Burns, Robert Murray M'Cheyne, George Müller, Adoniram Judson, and John G. Paton used similar language. But they described their experience of the joyful great exchange in the doctrine of union with Christ. Whether it was the assurance of Christ's righteousness or the security of union with Christ (both through *sola fide*), the great exchange has produced a happy fortitude for countless Great Commission servants.

This joyful great exchange is the foundation for long-term Great Commission spirituality and service. It doesn't burn out with workaholism or black out with indifference. It refreshes all those who labor in unknown fields, languishing under hidden burdens, and wondering if God will ever make good on his promises. We can serve with all the strength of Christ powerfully working in us: "I have been crucified with Christ. It is no longer I who live, but Christ who lives in me. And the life I now live in the flesh I live by faith in the Son of God, who loved me and gave himself for me" (Gal 2:20).

Our work in the Great Commission is not our work. It is work, to be sure, but it is Christ's work. All that we are and do is in Christ. As Paul said about his labor in Christ's service, "For this I toil, struggling with all his energy that he powerfully works within me" (Col 1:29). This is the power of a justified life. This is the power of a life united with Christ. This is the power of faith alone.

Knowing and abiding in this freedom in Christ—freedom from the self-imposed yoke of being and doing enough—establishes a glad-hearted

9 Burns, *Notes of Addresses*, 5. Emphasis in the original.

contentment that receives all our Father's sweet and severe providences with the faith, curiosity, and wonder of a child who heartily admires his dad. This spiritual secret of peaceful contentment is the key for plodding on and reaping a harvest for eternity. Paul describes it like this:

> I have learned in whatever situation I am to be content. I know how to be brought low, and I know how to abound. In any and every circumstance, I have learned the secret of facing plenty and hunger, abundance and need. I can do all things through him who strengthens me. (Phil 4:11–13)

Union with Christ Empowers Great Commission Spirituality

Many of us wonder what spiritual secret of blessings such renowned Great Commission servants have discovered. What manner of spirituality are they practicing? More than that, we worry that we have already missed our chance at achieving such blessings. It feels like time is against us. All those wasted years, it seems, have amounted to such paltry results: shallow and distant relationships, and spiritual famines when everyone else's harvests seem to increase abundantly, unimpressive times of prayer, and group Bible studies that feel more like demotivating pep talks.

We wonder what God expects of us. Do more or do less? Great Commission service seemed so exciting and promising when we first felt inspired to spend our life in Christ's service. What is the secret to that blessed life? Some say we need to surrender all and make Christ Lord of all. Others say we need to repent more and search out even our unintentional sins. While others say we must pray with true faith, claim God's promises, and bind the evil one. The list of possible solutions can seem endless. Many of those blessed saints seem to have their own set of access codes that unlocked the victorious Christian life. There seems to be something special about those who claim to walk with God and hear his voice all the time. It seems like they have unmediated access to God.

Great Commission spirituality should not be confused with the ascetic missionary spirituality of medieval Roman Catholic mysticism. Though not always the case, the writings of the monastics and their missionaries often demonstrate a fundamental confusion of union with Christ. Sometimes, well-intended men and women would deny themselves common comforts and pleasures to purge themselves of their sinful flesh, to fight the devil, to accomplish God's work with uncommon blessing and power, or to achieve the blessed state of union with Christ.

Typically, their ascetic, self-denying spirituality combined all these motivations. But sadly, these are not biblical motivations because they emerge from a confused notion of union with Christ. We don't achieve union with Christ and all his blessings through our faithfulness; we receive union with Christ and all his blessings through faith alone. From eternity past, God chose us in Christ to be adopted in love. All of heaven's spiritual blessings are ours to enjoy because of this inheritance which is only received through faith alone. The blessings are the applications of God's promises to us in Christ.

The common code language for the doctrine of union with Christ in the New Testament includes: *in Christ*, *in him*, *in God*, *in the Beloved*, and similar names. Consider how the Bible blends together the eternal security of our identity *in* Christ and all its promised (not potential) spiritual blessings.

God unilaterally ordained the blessings of our identity in Christ since before the creation of the world. They are not potentials for us to tap into based upon how radical, abandoned, and super spiritual we are. A contract stipulates potentials. A covenant secures promises. Notice the superlatives of how immeasurably secure we are in Christ from eternity past; notice how we receive God's lavish kindness in Christ with every heavenly blessing:

> Blessed be the God and Father of our Lord Jesus Christ, who has blessed us in Christ with every spiritual blessing in the heavenly places, even as he chose us in him before the foundation of the world, that we should be holy and blameless before him. In love he predestined us for adoptions as sons through Jesus Christ, according to the purpose of his will, to the praise of his glorious grace, with which he has blessed us in the Beloved. In him we have redemption through his blood, the forgiveness of our trespasses, according to the riches of his grace, which he lavished upon us, in all wisdom and insight. … In him we have obtained an inheritance, having been predestined according to the purpose of him who works all things according to the counsel of his will, so that we who were the first to hope in Christ might be to the praise of his glory. In him you also, when you heard the word of truth, the gospel of your salvation, and believed in him, were

> sealed with the promised Holy Spirit, who is the guarantee of our inheritance until we acquire possession of it, to the praise of his glory. (Eph 1:3–8, 11–14)

The Mystery of Life in Christ

Dissertations and volumes over the centuries have sought to shed light on the mystery of union with Christ. But it is inexhaustible. This doctrine belongs in a similar category with the Trinity—a doctrine of divine mystery that human language can never utterly define. The very terms *define* and *definition* are derived from the idea of the finite. Therefore, the infinite God blows apart all our definitional categories.

How can we define the indefinable? We can't. While we *can* define absolutely true things about God and our union in Christ—that is the very purpose of creeds and confessions—we cannot absolutely define God and our union in Christ. So any attempt to capture in words the excellencies of this doctrine must be humbly treated as just that—an attempt. God gives us earthly language that is sufficient to know him *partially* in his indescribable, sublime, and transcendent glory. Indeed, though we see through a glass dimly, we still see *truly*.

Being in Christ is not so much about what we do and how we function. It is more about who we are. It's not even an emphasis on union *with* Christ (which we typically say in English), though that is a lovely implication. It is union *in* Christ. It's new identity language. It's even different than a legal, forensic declaration. It is an organic, vibrant, vital sharing in the divine nature.

More than giving us life, Christ *is* our life. More than giving us peace, Christ *is* our peace. More than making us righteous, Christ *is* our righteousness. More than making us wise, Christ *is* our wisdom. More than making us pleasing to God, Christ *is* our honor. Identification in Christ is sufficient. To identify ourselves by our activity (e.g., acting wisely or living righteously) is to talk like we are separate from him. He did not merely share his attributes with us, giving us life, wisdom, peace, honor, and righteousness. He became those things *for* us, *in* us.

The believer's "with-in-ness" in Christ is certainly a mystery, and more than just a relationship. We don't just get benefits *from* him. His benefits are ours as much as they are his. All this because we are *in* him. And this is part of the heavenly mystery that God has designed earthly marriage to communicate: a wife, in a marital union with her husband, shares in all the benefits of her husband's name, reputation, earnings, and successes. Her shameful past now vanishes forever. She is free from that bondage by sharing in his good family name. Her bridegroom has bestowed his irresistible grace. Her only response? Receive him and rest in him. Her old reputation and life are gone. Her new reputation and life are in her husband's name. All the honor and blessings of his name are hers.

More accurately, Jesus and his people are in mystical union. We share in all of Christ and all the blessings he has secured through his redemptive work. This is not mysticism—in the spiritualist, esoteric, gnostic sense. Rather, this is a vital and mystical union.

Union and Communion in Christ's Service

This pastoral doctrine of union with Christ was a decisive truth that made me see the extravagant beauty of God's word, world, and works. Union with Christ transforms how we see into the ordinary and the extraordinary. And it establishes Great Commission service and spirituality. How so? Because we begin to see that all of creation, life, redemption, and eternity are about God lavishly bestowing the riches of his kindness upon his beloved people *in* Christ. That preposition is absolutely crucial. What does *in* Christ mean? It certainly does not mean locally in Christ, since we are physically on earth and Christ is physically reigning at the Father's right hand. But it is not merely a metaphor or an analogy. Neither is it merely instrumental (such as *by* or *with*). Instead, it suggests being within, among, or within the sphere of. Christ inundates and immerses us into a new identity altogether.

The New Testament uses "in Christ" or "in him" (referring to Christ) 180 times. In grammar it is nominal (substantive), taking the place of a noun, verb, or adjective. John uses the same kind of nominal grammar to say, "God is love" (1 John 4:8), not merely that God is loving. And John records Jesus claiming, "I am the truth" (John 14:6), not, "I am truthful."

Since we are justified through faith alone, life in Christ means that God takes pleasure in us (despite our shameful sins) in the same measure he takes pleasure in Christ (because of his honoring obedience). Christ supremely honored God through obedience to his law—loving God and others perfectly and truly. Therefore, God's pleasure in his begotten Son is eternal, immutable, and infinite. He declares over Christ: "This is my beloved Son, with whom I am well pleased" (Matt 3:17).

For each of us who are *in* Christ through faith alone, God looks at each of us with only pleasure and says, "this is my adopted son, in whom I am well pleased." We share in the firstborn Son's name and honor. Being *in* Christ secures unlimited access by the Spirit to the Father's praise, gladness, and approval. A perfectly honored God is our exceedingly great reward. We can neither improve nor diminish God's adoration for us in Christ. All this we receive through resting in Christ alone. This is the stuff of dreams, fables, and fairytales. But it is all true—the truest of true stories.

Tasting and digesting these truths nourishes us. Realizing how healthy they make our souls, we can rightly order our diet of all holy habits, spiritual disciplines, and ministry methods. Such habits, disciplines, and methods are important indeed, but they are not ultimate. They are like forks, knives, and cups—mere utensils for feasting on Living Bread and Water. What beggar bothers to admire and comment on the cutlery and so forgets to eat? Could our problems of burning out and blacking out be because we have been hungry for so long that we've stopped trying to eat? Maybe we have forgotten that we are actually hungry exiles and not special forces. Maybe we are too preoccupied with the ornate utensils that everyone commends. But feeding on our life in Christ through faith alone is the only way to receive strength and press on another day in his service. This is essential to Great Commission spirituality.

Already You Are Clean

Union with Christ for Great Commission spirituality might seem interesting but abstract. How does it concretely help us serve? How does it work to live life in Christ? What must we do? How is this book going to help us bear fruit in the Great Commission more than other books?

Isn't it interesting that we often go straight to the practical and functional question of what we must do to get what is promised? I confess I struggle with that. Why do we treat the promises as precepts? Why do we misread the truth statements as commands? Just as in the Beatitudes of Matthew 5:3–11, we often apply those "blesseds" as imperatives or conditions: "Be poor in spirit and then you will be blessed with the kingdom of heaven."

But these are indicatives of blessing, not imperatives for blessing. Standing on his mountain as the new Moses, Jesus is pronouncing the law's blessings upon those who receive him through faith alone. The Beatitudes are a New Covenant benediction of benevolence. We confuse this mountain (the figurative mountain of blessing) because we confuse two other mountains.

Sinai and Zion

Two mountains loom in the history of redemption. Mount Sinai represents the law of God and what we must do to achieve access to God. It provides the law's precepts and their potential blessings or curses. It's main imperative? Do. And like Israel at the base of Mount Sinai after receiving the law, we foolishly reply: "All this you require, we will do." But Zion is not like Sinai. Zion represents the grace of God and what he has done in the gospel to give free access to him in Christ. It bestows the blessings of the covenant's promises. It's main indicative? Done. And like those who wait on the Lord at the bottom of Mount Zion, we humbly reply: "In all this you have done, we trust."

The better question, now, is not "What must we do?" and not even, "Who must we be?" but rather, "What must be true?" What does it mean to abide in Christ? Abiding in Christ is a disposition relative to our new nature in Christ. It's more than a discipline to maximize our potential in Christ. When a foreign branch is spliced into a thriving vine, the cutting of the branch and its grafting onto the vine is not by the branch's power. The life-giving sap flowing into the fibers of the branch come from the vine alone. The root that drinks the water is of the vine alone. That once-foreign branch bears fruit because it takes on a new vital nature in the vine. The vine's function is to feed the branch with its life source. Through the branch, it pushes out the flower buds and the fruit.

Here we find liberation from the hamster-wheel Christianity that spins around and gets nowhere. Taylor brilliantly spelled out the relief of freedom from the spiritual-discipline treadmill. He recounts his joy at discovering the totality of our vital connection to Christ:

> As I thought of the Vine and the branches, what light the blessed Spirit poured direct into my soul! How great seemed my mistake in wishing to get the sap, the fullness out of Him! I saw not only that Jesus will never leave me, but that I am a member of His body,

> of His flesh and of His bones. The vine is not the root merely, but all—root, stem, branches, twigs, leaves, flowers, fruit. And Jesus is not that alone—He is soil and sunshine, air and showers, and ten thousand times more than we have ever dreamed, wished for or needed. Oh, the joy of seeing this truth![10]

Any command to abide in the Vine is a command to thrive according to our new nature in the Vine. Jesus said it this way: "Already you are clean because of the word that I have spoken to you" (John 15:3). The word for *clean*, here, is the same word as *pure* in the Beatitudes: "Blessed are the pure in heart" (Matt 5:8). He is referring to how the vinedresser cuts the branch from the deadness of its old root and grafts it into the cut-open side of the vine and secures it. Similarly, the Father has already cut us clean from death in Adam's guilt and corruption. Mirroring the blood and water that flowed from Christ's side for our redemption, so Christ's blood and water flows into our souls as we are grafted into his side and sealed with the Spirit's love. Faith in Christ is the instrument through which we receive new life in Christ.

All imperatives to abide in Christ grow out of indicatives about our union with Christ. They are like the very first imperative verb in Romans. Paul's first moral command to the Romans comes in chapter 6 after the previous five chapters of redemptive indicatives: "So you also must consider yourselves dead to sin and alive to God in Christ Jesus" (Rom 6:11). That first command in Romans immediately follows a reminder of our vital union in Christ:

> For if we have been united with him in a death like his, we shall certainly be united with him in a resurrection like his. We know that our old self was crucified with him in order that the body of sin might be brought to nothing, so that we would no longer be enslaved to sin. For one who has died has been set free from sin. (Rom 6:5–7)

In other words, the command to abide in Christ is not so much a prescription for a technique with a potential fruitful outcome. Rather, it is a reminder to rest in his strength no matter the season or the circumstance. Branches are fruitful and multiply because they are connected to the vine.

10 Taylor, *Hudson Taylor's Spiritual Secret*, 87.

It's what they are. It's their nature. Adam's creation mandate was to go into the world and be fruitful and multiply. The last Adam's new creation mission is to go into all the world and through his branches be fruitful and multiply.

A great burden of man-centered spiritualities hangs over the consciences of Great Commission servants. It guarantees to make us pure vessels in the Lord's hand if and only if we follow enough spiritual steps and submit to enough spiritual authority. But this is not how fruit-bearing through our identity in Christ works. We should be relieved, rather, that God is the promise-keeper even when we try to manufacture his promises with over-fertilized and bio-engineered synthetic fruit. All our attempts apart from resting in and receiving his grace are tasteless, fake, and without organic substance. Yet, inside many of us, there is a retort: "But we must do something, right?" Yes, but whatever we do derives its source of life and strength from its union with Christ. And it must accord with the word of Christ.

Taylor was asked later in life about his theology of abiding in Christ: "But are you always conscious of abiding in Christ?" The question implied that he must always have Christ on his mind in order to derive the benefits of Christ. It would be like a wife assuming she must always think of her marriage in order to enjoy the blessings of her husband's name, security, and overall care. Taylor's reply was simple and profound: "While sleeping last night … did I cease to abide in your home because I was unconscious of the fact?"[11] Our vitality in the Vine does not ultimately depend upon us doing anything apart from Christ. Yes, we respond to the nourishment of the Vine and bear fruit, but that response corresponds to our new nature and our new name. It is what we do because it is who we are.

Treefulness

The imagery of the anticipated Branch sweeps across the pages of Scripture. The prophets speak of a coming Branch, beautiful and glorious (Isa 4:2), a righteous Branch of David (Jer 33:15; Zech 3:8; 6:12–13). As Eve and Abraham anticipated a coming Seed (Gen 3:15; 12:3), so David would have a Seed (2 Sam 7:11–17). David had faith in and alluded to the future glory of this Seed in his final words: "For will [God] not cause to prosper all my

11 Taylor, 88.

help and my desire?" (2 Sam 23:5). The verb "to cause to prosper" means "to branch out."[12] And Isaiah wrote that "there shall come forth a shoot from the stump of Jesse, and a branch [Hebrew *netzer*] from his roots shall bear fruit" (Isa 11:1).

The Lord says in Zecheriah that "Branch" is even his name: "Behold, the man whose name is the Branch: for he shall branch out from his place, and he shall build the temple of the LORD. It is he who shall build the temple of the LORD and shall bear royal honor" (Zech 6:12–13) as both priest and king. And from which town does the Branch come? Nazareth (from *netzer*), which means "Branch Town." Eve's Seed promised to Abraham and to David has grown out of Nazareth. He has become the Branch that has prospered in the hand of the Lord. He is the help and desire of David (2 Sam 23:5). He is the help and desire of the nations (Hag 2:7). In vital union with that Branch, the faith-filled children of Abraham among the nations shall receive the fruit of his kingdom.

Here is a word picture that approximates our fruitful abiding in Christ in Great Commission service. I almost made it the title of this book. It is the idea of "treefulness." The term "fruitfulness" seems to have been overused or misused in recent decades, probably because so many of us are removed from agrarian lifestyles. We don't experience those seasonal rhythms of farming. To be sure, now there are ways to manufacture fake, artificial, simulated fruit with bioengineering and other chemical interventions. But that is not true, organic fruit as God designed it in the created order. Any simple farmer throughout history would tell us that life is in the seed, though dormant. Essential for its growth is a combination of good soil, rain, sun, and time (in addition to watching for the threats of birds, thieves, floodwaters, and harsh cold).

By nature, trees do what God designed them to do without fretting, striving, or failing. They just are treeful. According to their nature, as they soak up the rain and sunshine, they eventually bear fruit. Not because of what they do, but because of what they are. They are fruitful because they are treeful. Taylor described it this way: "Work is the outcome of effort; fruit, of life. A bad man may do good work, but a bad tree cannot bear good fruit."[13]

12 The noun form is "branch" as well.

13 Taylor, *Hudson Taylor's Spiritual Secret*, 149.

Great Commission spirituality would have a hollow ring if it did not underscore our organic growth by God's power through faith in his promises with virtue for effective fruit-bearing. Peter explains how the Bible grounds our life and fruitfulness in our life in Christ:

> His divine power has granted to us all things that pertain to life and godliness, through the knowledge of him who called us to his own glory and excellence, by which he has granted to us his precious and very great promises, so that through them you may become partakers of the divine nature, having escaped from the corruption that is in the world because of sinful desire. For this very reason, make every effort to supplement your faith with virtue, and virtue with knowledge, and knowledge with self-control, and self-control with steadfastness, and steadfastness with godliness, and godliness with brotherly affection, and brotherly affection with love. For if these qualities are yours and are increasing, they keep you from being ineffective or unfruitful in the knowledge of our Lord Jesus Christ. (2 Pet 1:3–8)

God has ordered our days as we grow up into his divine likeness. Our spiritual life and godliness find their source in God. He has granted us all we need to grow into perfect Christlikeness. What tool does he use to do that? His "precious and very great promises" (2 Pet 1:4). Being rooted through faith in those promises, we devote ourselves to maturing in virtue. Notice that Peter describes our spirituality as virtue rather than habit. Virtue is more of an inclination and mindset than it is a practice or behavior. Of course, we should act virtuously, but doing so presupposes that we have a virtuous nature. Otherwise, we are hypocrites and actors.

As we mature in the knowledge of Christ, we increase in virtue. Virtue is not measurable in quantity, but it is evident in quality. As seasons come and go, we can discern the health of the tree as it grows and produces more and better fruit. After a great drought, deep freeze, or windstorm, the growth of the tree may stagnate and suffer. But it is not dead or lost. It just needs extra care and nurture to regain its strength and bear fruit again. In Christ, the evidence of our Great Commission fruitfulness and effectiveness comes from God's power maturing us in virtue through resting in his promises. Christ's cross is the tree. Our Great Commission success is his fruit. Because of our union with him in death and in resurrection, his treefulness is our treefulness, and fruit-bearing is merely the natural consequence of our identity in him and his tree.

A Prayerful Instinct of Restfulness in Christ

My prayer is that this chapter encourages us to observe our fundamental motivations and perceived source of strength in Great Commission service. Why do we do what we do? On what basis do we assure ourselves that God will use us and bear fruit? Are we motivated by a commitment we made to God years ago in response to a heavy burden he placed on our souls? Are we motivated because the need is so great and the laborers so few?

Late at night, on December 31, when the final minutes are counting down, do all our regrets of the preceding 364 days discourage us? Do we remember our inadequacies as gospel servants? How do we cope? Resolve again to try harder for another year? Pray with more faith in the new year? Maybe something else. Whatever it is, my friend, remember Jesus Christ. He is our life. He will make good on his promises, whether we are strugglers like Samson or scoundrels like Jacob. Rest in Christ. It is his work. Every day.

> *The branch of the vine does not worry, and toil, and rush here to seek for sunshine, and there to find rain. No; it rests in union and communion with the vine; and at the right time, and in the right way, is the right fruit found on it. Let us so abide in the Lord Jesus.*
>
> —Hudson Taylor

Chapter 2

Prayer

Abiding in Christ and the Nearness of God

Scripture for Meditation:

The LORD is near to all who call on him, to all who call on him in truth.

—Psalm 145:18

Whether life is spilling over with singing and celebration or parched with sorrow and depression, the soul at rest in Christ says, "Whom have I in heaven but you? And there is nothing on earth that I desire besides you. My flesh and my heart may fail, but God is the strength of my heart and my portion forever. ... But for me it is good to be near God" (Ps 73:25–26, 28).

Some perceive such restful, content piety as a mere shade of personality. However, this is not an issue of personality profiles. Rather, this is what faith alone in Christ alone looks like. It is a hearty trust. A peaceful rest. True faith yields itself like a lamb to the Shepherd's care; whether he handles me with tenderness or hands me over to torture, whether he leads me beside still water or leads me to the slaughter, Jesus is enough for me. True faith abides in Christ and bears fruit accordingly. The instrument of our union with Christ is faith alone, and evidence of life in that union is a prayerful and fruitful faith.

Union with Christ is the essence of all that we are. It is our truest of true identities. And contrary to works-righteousness mysticism, union with Christ is the ground, not the goal, of our prayerfulness. We don't pray to achieve union with Christ and its blessings. We pray because we are already united to Christ. And in him we receive his blessings. This is what it means to be at rest in Christ. We have already entered his Sabbath rest.

If we don't understand who we are in Christ and what that union provides for us, then our prayers may seek to manipulate or impress God with our emotive intensity, routine fidelity, or self-assured purity. We can be tempted to read biblical passages about prayer and presume they are effective based upon our own degree of piety. Sometimes we decode God's extraordinary outpourings in revival history as a blueprint for what the Spirit would do in our day if and only if we imitate those anointed saints.

We tend to worry that God is withholding promised blessings unless we pray fervently, in unity, in community, with all faith and no doubting whatsoever. As a result, we may inadvertently put our faith in our sincerity and pure-hearted motives. We mobilize ourselves by claiming that the Lord's will for the church is clearly seen in the book of Acts. And if the church is not growing, multiplying, and seeing the signs and wonders of Acts, then we may assume something is wrong with us. We may think our inability to believe enough is quenching the Spirit's power. We admit that the church has not advanced spectacularly in the Great Commission since the first few centuries, and many of us conclude that this lack of progress is because of our faithlessness and spiritual weakness. For the Great Commission servant, such sentiments can be deadening and disheartening.

Prayer Formulas for Power

I've been serving in vocational missions since the early 2000s, and I have heard numerous diagnoses with corresponding prescriptions for reasons the church is not rapidly multiplying around the world like the early church. To be fair, I have swallowed and even passed around a few of these pills at times and found myself sickened.

Here are some common diagnoses: Some make comparisons and judgments based upon the perception of congregational worship in different cultures. One culture's worship seems subdued and pensive whereas another's seems vibrant and flush with emotion. Others compare the wealth of the church in one culture with the poverty of the church in another culture. Some propose that the wealthy church is dead while the impoverished church is imitating the way of Christ. Others claim that God has greatly blessed the wealthy church, implying that his blessings have strangely passed by the poorer church.

If we have served in the Great Commission, especially outside of our native culture or passport country, we know how tempting it is to make these comparisons. By doing so, we treat God's promises as though they are potentials. We might declare that we must pray and "claim the promises" or "lay hold of the promises." We can quickly turn prayer and prayer-empowered service into some sort of passcode to unlock the encrypted blessings of God for us to finish the Great Commission. It can feel like God is waiting up in heaven with a storehouse of promises: joy, blessings, and power to complete the Great Commission. It can all be ours now, it seems, if we discern his secret will, listen intently for his ambiguous promptings, and act upon them with reckless faith and sincere surrender.

Prescriptions, Prayer, and Power

Here are some common solutions we might prescribe for the diagnosis of an impaired, chronically fatigued church with heart disease: Regular doses of unity, simplicity, purity, and fervency.

The prescription is hardly one small pill to swallow. If we're honest, we sometimes assume only the early church and occasional short-lived historical revivals have followed the doctor's orders to the letter. Yet, we must be cautious of those proposed ministry methods (e.g., church-planting techniques, innovative prayer practices). They often develop out of statistical conversion rates, anecdotes, and quantitative data from census bureau reports.

Headcounts, spectacular stories, and census reports don't tell the full story. Rarely do researchers of quantitative data have the opportunity to study the qualitative evidence of a revival's actual biblical fruitfulness over time. Many censuses record whole villages as Christian simply because those villages have a Catholic church building, or some villagers celebrate Christmas, or once attended a wedding in a church building. Researchers may hear legends of an itinerant band of evangelists that traveled through that region years prior, so now the census bureau reports that whole village as Christian.

Consequently, methodologies can emerge based upon the alleged spiritual practices of those revivalists—home Bible studies, city-wide prayer vigils, dreams and visions, women evangelists, telling Jesus stories, deliverance prayer, etc. Did those things happen? Possibly. Does data report a higher percentage of Christians years or even months later? Potentially. But watch out for the *post hoc* logical fallacy—*y* followed *x*; therefore, *x* caused *y*. And be alert to the other common fallacy that claims, "correlation implies causation." It should be said, though, that we don't need to be suspicious of every exciting report. We should indeed be hopeful and optimistic. But the point is, we shouldn't be discouraged when we can't seem to tap into God's special power for God's special servants. Long-term biblical fruitfulness is the best qualitative evidence of God at work. Not anecdotes and headcounts.

Some anecdotes of such unverifiable accounts have become sacred legends influencing the methodologies of generations of Great Commission organizations. Typically, the proposed prognosis is good: we can experience a revived healthy church that transforms the world, as we align ourselves with how the Spirit has worked in the past. The assumption is, the Spirit is willing to move like in the book of Acts. And we must decipher what to do and what to pray so he will move powerfully. If we don't press in enough, some think he will pass by our Great Commission efforts. That's one reason why "movement" terminology is so popular in mission organizations. A catalytic movement is the perceived evidence that the Spirit is indeed working.

So many of us with "boots on the ground" feel pressure to keep up with the Spirit's patterns of power from both the past and the present. It can feel like everyone else has a dynamic ministry but us. It's draining. But that exhaustion, we often presume, is because something is wrong with us. We feel like we haven't pressed hard enough into the Spirit's power. Our conferences and trainings don't always help either. Sometimes that's when we hear the motivational calls to walk in lockstep with the Spirit together in city-wide prayer, catalyzing rapid disciple-making movements. To be fair, my own theological immaturity and zeal led me to propose similar things in the past. It's easy to do. Yet God is patient with our misdirected sincerity. Like Jesus with Peter, he can steer our impetuous passion.

Here are common features of the prescribed spiritual formulae:

- **Unity**: let us put aside our differences and unite (the assumption is that denominations and traditions quench the Spirit's power).
- **Simplicity**: let us guard our hearts with a child-like simplicity of love for Jesus (the assumption is that Jesus unites and doctrine divides).
- **Purity**: let us scour our conscience for any residual unconsecrated desire and unholy motive (the assumption is that God is waiting to answer our prayers once we have surrendered all with our whole hearts).
- **Fervency**: in all our devotion to the prescription, let us follow the doctor's orders with impassioned prayers (the assumption is that anything less than radical zeal would indicate that we are lukewarm Christians, which Jesus spits out).

I have witnessed elder board meetings where the whole board voted in favor of a decision related to missions. But one elder suspended the decision because he felt a "check in his spirit." This one dissenting voice prevented them from unanimously moving ahead for fear of quenching the Spirit through disunity. In the end, they all gave up. They feared walking out of the Lord's umbrella of protection and blessing. I have seen church-planting efforts with missionaries who esteem listening-prayer. They explicitly suspend teaching Scripture altogether because they caution that authoritative Bible teaching is pharisaical and puts God in a box.

Ironically, in our eagerness to hear God's voice, we can insinuate that biblical teaching silences the Spirit and discourages the child-like faith that Jesus commends for a simple church. If the Bible is used, we too often use it is a tool for ensuring better obedience and preventing the loss of power. I have received advice (and regrettably, I have given the same advice a few times before) that we are not ready for Great Commission service until we crucify every impure motive and thought. And this readiness only comes when we are consciously seeking the filling of the Spirit. If we feel sexual attraction, have an unrighteous angry moment, or entertain a secret desire for pleasing people, then we are unfit for God's service—even if these are mere anomalies and not chronic patterns. Surely, many assume, God wouldn't use a dirty vessel.

I have read sociological missions books that suggest the reason there has been an explosion of church growth in the Global South is because they pray and worship with fervency. The strong implication is that unemotional churches in the Global North are devoid of the Spirit's power in worship. It's even implied that such churches may be spiritually dead.

Yet, the sociologists rarely admit that in most of those same Global South cultures where church worship is strikingly animated, such expressiveness corresponds to other cultural practices. Many of their pre-Christian religions, new religious movements, and prosperity gospel cults, also exude a similar fervor. Such soulfulness might be more culturally ingrained than spiritually anointed.

Not to mention that the same secret sins of lying, sexual immorality, corruption, spiritual abuse, pride, and gossip are sadly prevalent in churches of every culture. Secret sins do not diminish based upon passion, seriousness, and sincerity. It's a human problem unrelated to our temperaments and worship styles. Our composure in congregational Sunday worship does not limit our temptations and old sin nature. Just as God made birds, fish, and animals to be beautifully varied, he made languages and peoples to be diverse. Different is good. God likes it that way, or else he would have made us identical. The good news is, God has no favorites. He loves his children—male or female, rich or poor, Jew or gentile, passionate or pensive—all the same in Christ.

Honestly and humbly acknowledging our cultural differences in respect to prayer is a healthy step toward remembering our true spiritual identity. It is in Christ alone. Not in our cultural worship expressions. Not in our perceived prayer power. Our worship styles, prayer practices, and perceived power are not true indicators of how God is pleased with us. He sees us in Christ alone. We add nothing to the power of Christ's word. More enthusiasm does not mean more effectiveness. More quietness does not mean more holiness. The power is in our union with Christ, not our piety or passion.

Praying in Christ to a Good Promise-Giving God

Why are prayer as a discipline and prayerfulness as a disposition both so difficult to maintain? Could it be that we have an overwhelming number of methods and an underwhelming amount of motivation? Like New Years resolutions for improved health, we start off strong but grow weary with time. We find our new habits don't produce what we anticipated.

Here is the strange irony: we often languish for lack of nutrition. Many of us are malnourished because we have given up on eating. The initial hunger pangs are gone, and we have become complacent in our starved state. We have been hungry for years. We have forgotten what it is like to be full. For too long we have tolerated a persistently empty soul. Or, maybe worse, we have become malnourished because we have been eating contaminated food. "Why do you spend your money for that which is not bread, and your labor for that which does not satisfy? Listen diligently to me, and eat what is good, and delight yourselves in rich food" (Isa 55:2). Our taste buds have dulled—we are willing to consume anything as long as it deadens the hunger pangs. In some of the countries where I have ministered, I have seen children who live in garbage heaps. They will eat glue and plastic just to kill the hunger and sniff gasoline for a cheap buzz and the feeling of a full belly to sleep at night.

Dear friend, why do we languish unnecessarily in the Lord's service? He *gives* us promises—good promises. He even grants us the faith and repentance necessary to receive new life and rest in those promises (cf. Acts 11:18; 16:14; Eph 2:8–9; Phil 1:29; 2 Tim 2:25). Our God doesn't just promise a successful Great Commission; he promises to be with us in Christ every step of the way. He doesn't just promise strength for the task. He promises that his joy in Christ will be our strength. He doesn't just promise us a reward in the end. He is himself our promised very great reward in Christ.

Jesus is not waiting for us to get busy and activate his promises with enough spiritual discipline, passionate prayer, faithfulness in ministry, and abandoned surrender to him. Jesus does not dangle the promises out in front of us as a bait if only we would reach out hard enough and lay hold of them. Jesus does not trick his people with prophetic puzzles, elusive whispers, and encrypted impressions if only we would lean in and discover their hidden message. He doesn't play games with us. Jesus loves his servants. And he has sworn with his life to guide us by his counsel and bring us home to glory.

Praying in Christ to a Faithful Promise-Keeping God

Here is where we assuage all the anxiety that we subconsciously feel when trying to do enough to claim God's promises. The Bible does not teach that God's promises are potentials. They are received through faith alone in Christ alone by grace alone. They are not achieved by sincere faithfulness to spiritual prescriptions in addition to the Spirit's assisting grace. Promises do not rely upon sufficiently obeyed prescriptions. And these promises are not like receiving a miracle cure and then maintaining good health with sufficient devotion to a diet and exercise plan. We don't receive God's promises in part at conversion through faith and then achieve them incrementally through our faithfulness. The promises are not for us to access finally in eternity to the degree we followed their spiritual prescriptions.

That is not how the New Covenant in Christ works. In Christ's death, God enacted a covenant for his people by himself. Because of Christ's new life, God keeps the covenant for his people by himself. For, "If we are faithless, he remains faithful—for he cannot deny himself" (2 Tim 2:13). In the law, God *prescribes* righteousness for our good, yet in Adam we fall short to our shame. But in Christ, God *promises* righteousness for our good, and upon that grace we stand to his honor. What God commands in the law, he gives in Christ. All of God's promises are ours in Christ. And God hears and answers our prayers according to his promises in Christ. God has sworn by his name, and he will not back down from his promise to uphold the honor of his grace (cf. Isa 48:9; Ezek 20:44). To do so would be to take his name in vain.

God will give Christ the nations as his inheritance: "Ask of me, and I will make the nations your heritage, and the ends of the earth your possession" (Ps 2:8). And he will give to Christ a people to be with him and see his glory: "Father, I desire that they also, whom you have given me, may be with me where I am, to see my glory that you have given me because you loved me before the foundation of the world" (John 17:24).

The amazing thing about both of those passages is that they are promises for Christ according to his prayers. When we pray in Christ for our Great Commission service by his power through us, we can rest assured that God's promises to Christ include us as well. God's promises to Abraham—to bless the nations through his Seed—are for us as well. In fact, we are all part of the nations redeemed in Christ as promised to Abraham. By faith, like Abraham, we are in Christ and share in all his inheritance (Eph 1:11–18).

Praying in Christ to such a promise-keeping God is the most secure position in the universe. We can pray with confidence resting assured that God is bestowing all his promises upon us in Christ:

> For all the promises of God find their Yes in him. That is why it is through him that we utter our Amen to God for his glory. And it is God who establishes us with you in Christ, and has anointed us, and who has also put his seal on us and given us his Spirit in our hearts as a guarantee. (2 Cor 1:20–22)

The Bible warns against the presumption of making promises to God, since we don't even know what tomorrow holds. God denounces any declaration about what we will do in the future as evil if we do not qualify it with, "if the Lord wills, we will live and do this or that" (Jas 4:15–16). Our God reserves all the power and deserves all the praise for keeping covenant with his unfaithful people. So, when we pray, we pray to this promise-keeping God. Since we are in Christ, he delights in us with an eternal, infinite, and immutable love.

Though we labor in his harvest, he is the Lord of the harvest. Though our labor in this cursed world seems burdensome, it is not utterly burdensome. It is a peaceful battling, a plodding stillness, marked by glad-hearted contentment and confidence in Christ. Prayer is calling upon the Lord of the harvest to do his will.

Praying in Christ to an Omniscient, Omnipotent God

The great rock of assurance in Great Commission spirituality is that our God is omnipotent, omniscient, and in absolute control. He smiles favorably on us and beckons us to draw near to his throne of grace. Every beat of a bee's wing, every flicker of a dust particle, every explosive thunderclap, every softly laid snowflake, every birth of a star, every twitch of a grass blade, every twist of a worm, every flat tire, every signature of a politician, every hand in Las Vegas, and every chirp of a bird is by God, from God, and for God. That same loving Creator is our Father, and he adores his children. This reality should amplify our prayers and not silence them.

Since God is sovereign, why pray? For the same reason we should share the gospel: because God is sovereign. He has commanded it, and that is enough. Just as he ordained the salvation of sinners, he has ordained evangelism for bringing about their conversion. Similarly, God ordains his help, power, and miracles through the means of prayer. Prayer is a link in the chain of God's ordained events. God wills that we eat in order to thrive; he also wills that we pray in order to bear fruit. Prayer is the branch drinking the sap of the Vine. The blood of the Vine courses through the branch's veins and slowly issues buds, flowers, and fruit.

Consider this: the Almighty God, maker, and sustainer of all things, both visible and invisible, calls us his adopted sons, and we call him our Father. He welcomes us to commune with him and cast our cares upon him. What an amazing privilege. We get to draw near with boldness to this God. Why would we even hesitate to come to our Almighty Father in heaven?

The Heidelberg Catechism provides a fabulous commentary on the first line of the Apostles' Creed about the almightiness of God our Father. Question twenty-six asks, "What do you believe when you say, 'I believe in God, the Father Almighty, Maker of heaven and earth?'" The answer fleshes out the comfort we enjoy in Christ—our standing with our good, wise, and sovereign Father is perfectly secure:

> That the eternal Father of our Lord Jesus Christ, who of nothing made heaven and earth with all that is in them, who likewise upholds, and governs them by His eternal counsel and providence, is for the sake of Christ, His Son, my God and my Father, in whom I so trust as to have no doubt that He will provide me with all things necessary for body and soul; and further, that whatever evil He sends upon me in this valley of tears, He will turn to my good; for He is able to do it, being Almighty God, and willing also, being a faithful Father.[1]

Consider where Hudson Taylor derived his assurance in prayer. He held fast to the security of his Father's wise, benevolent sovereignty over him. He knew the Father listened to his prayers for his mission work because he was "really one with a risen and exalted Saviour."[2] Taylor viewed

1 *Three Forms*, Kindle Edition, Location 1299.

2 Taylor, *Hudson Taylor's Spiritual Secret*, 87.

his membership in Christ as the source for power in prayer for Great Commission service:

> Again, think of its [that is, union with Christ] bearing on prayer. Could a bank clerk say to a customer, "It was only your hand, not you that wrote that check"; or "I can not pay this sum to your hand, but only to yourself"? No more can your prayers or mine be discredited if offered in the name of Jesus (i.e., not for the sake of Jesus merely, but on the ground that we are His, His members) so long as we keep within the limits of Christ's credit—a tolerably wide limit! If we ask for anything unscriptural, or not in accordance with the will of God, Christ Himself could not do that. ...
>
> The sweetest part ... is the rest which full identification with Christ brings. I am no longer anxious about anything, as I realise this; for He, I know, is able to carry out His will, and His will is mine. It makes no matter where He places me, or how. That is rather for Him to consider than for me; for in the easiest position He must give me His grace, and in the most difficult His grace is sufficient. It little matters to my servant whether I send him to buy a few cash worth of things, or the most expensive articles. In either case he looks to me for the money and brings me his purchases. So, if God should place me in serious perplexity, must He not give much guidance; in positions of great difficulty, much grace; in circumstances of great pressure and trial, much strength? No fear that His resources will prove unequal to the emergency! And His resources are mine, for He is mine, and is with me and dwells in me.[3]

Instead of demotivating us to pray and proclaim the gospel, the sovereignty of God is the believer's only hope. Because we are in Christ and members of his body, God is our Father. Christ is the begotten Son of God, and we are in him as adopted sons of God and co-heirs. Such a kind, wise, sovereign God welcomes us to draw near in faith.

Praying in Christ and Abiding in His House

Here is a limited analogy of how union with an all-knowing, all-powerful Christ should stimulate our desire and longings for communion with him:

---

3 Taylor, 87–88.

abiding in Christ can be like living at home with him. He wields his infinite power to protect us and provide for us. He applies his infinite wisdom to lavish us with benevolence and abundance. Christ's perfect power protects us from the elements, the wild, and intruders. Christ's power also gives us light, keeps us warm, and makes us food. Christ's perfect knowledge sees our needs before we even ask and produces the best nourishment for our growth. He creates the atmosphere of a joyful home and the culture of an endearing family to give us what our hearts want most—belonging.

Some people speak of Christ being our foundation, which is true and good. But he is more than that. When constructing a house or a barn, the foundation is the most critical part. If the foundation is faulty, everything declines and deconstructs. But, no one walks into a house and exclaims, "Wow, this foundation is great!" We admire the architectural design, the craftsmanship, and the interior design. We enjoy how a house facilitates experiences of joy, security, comfort, feasting, laughter, nurture, hygiene, and rest. An animal's habitat is in the wild. But every culture knows that a human belongs with family. A family needs an abode that ensures not merely survival, but abundant life. An animal exists in a habitat; a human abides in a home.

Abiding in Christ is like dwelling in a home and enjoying it for all that it is. Jesus is not just the foundation; Jesus is everything. Jesus is the frame, the rebar, the roof, the walls, the door, the windows, the electricity, the water, the furniture, the food, the pictures, the music, and the overall happiness of knowing God. Jesus shelters and guards us. He warms and feeds us. Jesus refreshes and cleanses us. He teaches and listens to us. Jesus is our rest. Jesus is our song and our joy. He decorates our rooms with good memories, lest we forget all that he has done for us. His love fills us with all the fullness of God. Jesus is our all.

These analogies illustrate the truths of what it is like to enjoy abiding in Christ. They are the rights and privileges of the adopted sons of God. In this life, we enjoy our union in part. But in the resurrection, Christ will be ours without measure, without end, and without change. United to Christ, we prayerfully sip from a small cup in this age. In the new creation, we will be swallowed up into an ocean of God's grace. Day after day. Age after age.

Whether we feel like rotten sinners or self-righteous hypocrites, our prayer-hearing God always welcomes those who call upon him in Christ. Always. Our practice of prayer in Great Commission service can become incredibly life-giving. We should pray that the Lord would help us see into the seemingly abstract doctrine of union with Christ. May we see it concretely for all its loveliness.

God's People and Their Prayerful Instinct

Sadly, many of us don't realize how important prayer is. Or we don't believe it really matters at the end of the day. What is worse, some of us operate by guilt-based motivations, so we try praying more because we feel disappointed in ourselves for our lack of consecrated piety. A better motivation for prayer comes by remembering that, because we are united to Christ, our God hears us when we call out to him. Unlike the gods of the pagans, our God answers prayer. It's common to say that prayer is powerful. But truly, God is powerful. Therefore, we call upon the name of the Lord.

If we are weak in prayer, we tend to be weak everywhere. Prayer is one of the most faith-filled things we can do. Prayer seems ineffective because we often equate effectiveness with busyness. But, in reality, prayer is when faith is most active—calling upon a God we cannot see to accomplish things we cannot do. It asks for abiding strength to act upon his promises. Sometimes it might feel like God has answered our prayers insufficiently. Yet, if he does not give us what we call for, he will certainly give us something even better. Better than we know to ask or imagine. And whatever that is, we will see its ultimate fulfillment in our union with Christ in the resurrection.

Satan knows how to twist Scripture. He may deceive us: "God knows what you need; you don't need to call out. You don't need to pray for power to preach the gospel. You don't need to confess your sins." It's true that God knows what we need, so that is why we shouldn't be anxious. But, when we are anxious or in need of help, we are commanded to pray. Satan knows that the weapon of our warfare is the word of God, which prayer wields with power.

Prayer is the strong arm that thrusts the sword of the word. The Bible says, "Take the helmet of salvation, and the sword of the Spirit, which is the word of God, praying at all times in the Spirit, with all prayer and supplication" (Eph 6:17–18). In other words, pray Scripture! But, since we are earthy people who like tangible results, we prefer to be clever and innovative, to read a book, start a committee, take a class, turn on the computer, Google our problem, or talk to a friend. We try anything first before calling upon the name of the Lord. That's exactly the enemy's tactic, especially for those on the frontlines of Great Commission service.

Prayer was the pattern of Jesus's ministry and the lifeblood of the early church. The Gospel writers recorded only one instance where Jesus's followers directly asked him to teach them to do something; it was "Lord, teach us to pray" (Luke 11:1). We have no record of them asking, "teach us to cast out demons, do miracles, plant churches, walk on water, or be leaders." They had never witnessed anything like the devotion, warmth, urgency, and power of Jesus's prayer life. When Jesus cleansed the temple, he quoted Scripture: "My house shall be called a house of prayer" (Matt 21:13). He frequently slipped away at night to call upon his Father. Even the early church was born in a pattern of devout, continual prayer: "All these with one accord were devoting themselves to prayer, together with the women and Mary the mother of Jesus, and his brothers" (Acts 1:14). They were praying when the Spirit came. Prayerfulness was their instinct, their nature. The people of God instinctively call upon him.

Calling Upon the Name of the Lord

After Adam sinned, two kinds of people would emerge—the righteous and the wicked, or as Augustine called them, the "City of God" and the "City of Man."[4] The people devoted to the heavenly kingdom (the righteous ones) are described as those who live by faith alone, those who fear God, and those who call upon the name of the Lord. The people devoted to the worldly kingdoms (the wicked ones) are described as those who do not trust the Lord, those who do not fear God, and those who do not call upon the name of the Lord.

What does it mean to call upon the name of the Lord? Depending on the context in Hebrew and Greek, to call upon the name of the Lord "means to proclaim or praise the excellence of Yahweh, to worship Yahweh, or to summon Yahweh by name for help."[5] The Bible teaches that those who call upon the name of the Lord are saved. And those who are saved continue to call upon the name of the Lord. Just like those who trust in the Lord are

4 Augustine, *City of God*.

5 Mounce, *Mounce's Complete Expository Dictionary*, 2145 [#7924].

declared righteous, the righteous continue to trust in the Lord. And a life of calling upon the name of the Lord is a chief expression of that continual trust in the Lord.

Sometime during the life of Enosh (grandson of Adam), the people of God instinctively began to call upon his name. Drawing near to Yahweh in prayer was different than calling on any other god. This God answered when they called out. The true people of God were marked by calling upon his name: "To Seth also a son was born, and he called his name Enosh. At that time people began to call upon the name of the LORD" (Gen 4:26). And throughout the rest of Old Testament, the righteous are distinguished by this practice of calling upon his name: "They will call on my name, and I will answer them. I will say, 'They are my people'; and they will say, 'The LORD is my God'" (Zech 13:9; cf. Ps 34:15–17).

Conversely, the wicked are described as those who will not call upon the name of the Lord: "Pour out your anger on the nations that do not know you, and on the kingdoms that do not call upon your name" (Ps 79:6; cf. Ps 14:4; Jer 10:25). Yet God promises to hear and draw near to his saints who call upon his name: "The LORD is near to all who call on him, to all who call on him in truth" (Ps 145:18; cf. Pss 50:15–16; 56:9; 86:5–7; 91:15; 116:2).

Moreover, there is an evangelistic element to calling upon the name of the Lord. The God of the Bible, when called upon in the name of Christ, answers our prayers. No other god, spirit, or ancestor can do this. In Great Commission service, I have learned from hilltribe pastors that one of the best tools for evangelism in their villages is praying for unbelievers. When those prayers to Christ are answered, those unbelieving animists, Buddhists, Muslims, and Hindus will often trust in Christ as their true God. Never before have they witnessed a God who answers the simple prayers of his people.

Even in the Old Testament, the identity of the God of Israel was distinguished from the gods of the nations because he answered prayer: "For what great nation is there that has a god so near to it as the LORD our God is to us, whenever we call upon him?" (Deut 4:7). No other ruler, emperor, king, or monarch would stoop to hear common people call upon him. But the Creator of the universe hears. He delights to answer our prayers. And when unbelievers see that, they are speechless (cf. 1 Kgs 18:24–27, 36–39; 1 Chr 16:8).

Calling Upon Christ in the New Testament

Another fascinating feature of calling upon the name of the Lord is how it naturally carries over into the identity and life of the New Testament church. The early Christians were described as those who call upon the name of the Lord: "Here [Saul] has authority from the chief priests to bind all who call on your name" (Acts 9:14); and "And all who heard [Paul] were amazed and said, 'Is not this the man who made havoc in Jerusalem of those who called upon this name?'" (Acts 9:21).

The saints are also described as those who call upon his name: "To the church of God that is in Corinth, to those sanctified in Christ Jesus, called to be saints together with all those who in every place call upon the name of our Lord Jesus Christ, both their Lord and ours" (1 Cor 1:2); "So flee youthful passions and pursue righteousness, faith, love, and peace, along with those who call on the Lord from a pure heart" (2 Tim 2:22).

In Romans 10:12, Paul argues that in Christ there is no distinction between Jew and gentile, because Jesus hears them call upon him and answers with equal abounding riches. He goes on to quote the common verse from the Old Testament that promises salvation for anyone who calls on his name: "Everyone who calls on the name of the Lord will be saved" (Rom 10:13). But the most surprising part of his argument is the next verse: "How then will they call on him in whom they have not believed? And how are they to believe in him of whom they have never heard? And how are they to hear without someone preaching?" (Rom 10:14). What is he assuming about the nature of calling upon the name of the Lord for believers? Unbelievers (and believers too) cannot have faith apart from hearing the word of Christ (Rom 10:17). And that word must come through a preacher. But what are people unable to do until they have believed? Verse 14 gives us the answer.

Until they have believed, people cannot call upon the name of the Lord. This means that calling upon the name of the Lord is not merely the common sinner's prayer—the unbeliever's response to the gospel message. Calling upon the name of the Lord is not just the key to unlock conversion. Calling upon the name of the Lord is the exclusive *privilege* that born-again souls have in Christ.

In Christ we can freely access and boldly draw near to God. Whether we are Jews or gentiles, praying to God is our inheritance. It's our royal honor as adopted sons in Christ. Paul is saying that once we preach the gospel and the nations believe, *they get to pray to their God and their Father*! Paul is echoing the effects of the promised conversion of the nations: "For at that time I will change the speech of the peoples to a pure speech, *that all of them may call upon the name of the LORD* and serve him with one accord" (Zeph 3:9).[6] Paul's message is: Preach the gospel so that the nations can draw near in Christ to the Father. The nearness of God is the ultimate good for all peoples.

If one aspect is regularly lacking in Great Commission spirituality, it is prayer. As the initial romance and idealism of ministry fade, many of us tire and grow slack in calling upon the name of the Lord. What other sin is so great than to spurn the extraordinary love of God? But God mercifully waits for us to draw near. He will never abandon or turn us away in Christ. For the sake of the Great Commission and the joy of our souls, let us pray for a fresh sight into the love of God, a revival of affection for Christ: "Give us life, and we will call upon your name" (Ps 80:18).

In Christ, we can regain our strength and remember the unending benefits of our union with Christ: "Come, everyone who thirsts, come to the waters; and he who has no money, come, buy and eat! Come, buy wine and milk without money and without price. ... Seek the LORD while he may be found; call upon him while he is near" (Isa 55:1, 6).

Unprayed Prayers Already Answered

It's not uncommon to lament the silence of God and our unanswered prayers. It's easy to grow weary over those prayers that seem to linger without noticeable fulfillment. We are so quick to put God on trial for why he "doesn't keep his promises," as though we always deserve a forthright reason for why we don't get our way.

Fortunately, as we mature, we become less presumptuous. As a result, however, we often become more apathetic. We've been disappointed so often in the past that it sometimes feels too painful or pointless to pray. We pray for the salvation of a language group. But God doesn't respond in ways that we notice. What's the point? But it doesn't need to be this way. God is so kind to us that he often prepares answers to our prayers before we utter them. Before we even know to utter them. It is impossible

6 Emphasis added.

to exhaustively know God in his eternality and infinitude. It is equally impossible to conceptualize how this God answers our prayers even before a word is on our tongue.

The story of Abraham seeking a wife for his son Isaac is one such account. The promise-giving God has vowed a Seed in whom all the nations would be blessed. That Seed must come through Isaac, which means Isaac must have sons. Here we have God giving a good promise of the coming Messiah. And Abraham heartily receives and rests in the promised Seed.

In Genesis 24, Abraham sends his servant back to Mesopotamia to find a wife for Isaac. The servant prays for the Lord to make clear who might be suitable. He asked that God would make the woman offer him a drink and water for his camels. Before the servant finished his prayer, a woman was coming. Rebekah had already been making her way to the well. And it says, "Before he had finished speaking [in prayer], behold, Rebekah, who was born to Bethuel the son of Milcah, the wife of Nahor, Abraham's brother, came out with her water jar on her shoulder" (Gen 24:15).

Whether the servant understood the magnitude of God's promise to Abraham, we don't know. But we should at least assume the servant had enough sense to fear Abraham's God as his master did. We know this because he does indeed pray on his own initiative. He then praises Yahweh for his steadfast love and faithfulness (Gen 24:27). Even here, God is so pleased to perform his promises, that he is sending the answer to this unnamed servant's prayer before the servant finishes it.

This illustrates the breathtaking security of praying in Christ according to God's will in Scripture. God is eager to send answers to our unfinished prayers. He will even start the answers to as yet unprayed prayers as they connect with his promises. In my own life, I have met big needs, threats, and obstacles on the mission field. I immediately called upon the Lord for help. Within twenty-four hours I learned that God's answer to those prayers were put in motion many days before I even had such a need.

God, in his eternality and omniscience, is there before us, with us, and behind us: "Before they call I will answer; while they are yet speaking I will hear" (Isa 65:24). He hears us because we are in vital union with Christ. And Christ mediates, advocates, and intercedes for us. As we pray according to his will, he hears the pleasing, beloved, honorable voice of his only begotten Son.

A Prayerful Instinct of Calling Upon the Name of Christ

The task of serving Christ in his Great Commission is not merely like a king stooping to give his sealed message to a beggar, granting him the honor of a "sent one." No, it's more than that. This King is the Creator of the world. He is King of kings. He is the infinite, immutable, eternal Son of God. He not only sends us out, but he promises to go with us. He promises to strengthen us, speak through us, and intercede for us. And he promises to advocate for us against the accuser. We get to share in the dignity, honor, and joy of his work. What is more, this King rewards us in the resurrection. He rewards us for the work that *he himself* accomplished through us. Jesus loves his people.

We get to take the King's message to the remotest edges of his empire. We get to watch him slowly expand his kingdom through the announcement of his victory. Of all people, Great Commission servants should be the most prayer-filled and hopeful. Our whole mission is based upon the promises of God. God has promised to give the nations to the Messiah, and we get to participate in his great mission. This promise is imperishable. It cannot fail.

God has granted all authority in heaven and on earth to Christ. By his name he will see to it that his servants will make disciples of every tribe, tongue, and nation. To be sure, all his servants struggle and fail to some degree. Yet through faith, they receive the promises. Not because of their faithfulness and fidelity to hold onto the promises. But because of God's faithfulness and fidelity to hold onto them and so empower them to prayerfully hope in the promises. Great Commission spirituality bears fruit through a prayerful instinct that regularly seeks God in Christ through the Spirit, with the promises in God's written word.

The history of missions is the history of answered prayer.

—Samuel Zwemer

Chapter 3

Meditation

Abiding in Christ with God's Word

Scripture for Meditation

> If you keep my commandments, you will abide in my love, just as I have kept my Father's commandments and abide in his love. These things I have spoken to you, that my joy may be in you, and that your joy may be full.
>
> —John 15:10–11

Martin Luther famously asserted that the biblical spirituality of a pastor-theologian should include three principles from Psalm 119: *oratio* (Prayer, v. 146); *meditatio* (Meditation, vv. 15, 27, 48); and *tentatio* (Affliction, vv. 67, 71). Similarly, Great Commission spirituality that feeds and forms the missionary-theologian incorporates this threefold framework.

Affliction tempts God's servants with anxiety about the trustworthiness of God's wisdom, love, and sovereignty. But through prayer and meditating on the promises of God in Christ, the Great Commission servant experiences assurance in Christ alone. In Christ, we don't establish our assurance—God has already secured that for us in our union with Christ before the creation of the world. Rather, in Christ we enjoy our assurance that God has freely promised us. Prayerfulness and Bible intake amidst the relentless struggle of Great Commission service are what we use to feed our souls. In Christ, God prepares a table for Great Commission servants. We can rest, eat, and get to work.

Of all the disciplines of the Christian life that offer the rest, refreshment, and renewal to endure in Great Commission service, our regular practice of Bible intake falls short more than most. We will practice a new prayer technique, imbibe another book on implementing sacred rhythms and holy habits, break away on a spiritual retreat, attend a class, observe a short fast, or even travel to a conference to hear our favorite preachers wax eloquent *about* the Bible.

Yet, how many of us regularly come to the fountain and drink for ourselves? Who among us feeds on God's word like our daily food? Are we malnourished for lack of access? Do we not have the Bible in our own language? Or maybe we have never truly understood how the word of Christ revives our souls. If we do take in the word, many of us take it as though we are not in Christ. We know intellectually that Christ has saved us and someday will finally save us. But as we read Scripture, we forget how vital our union is in him.

With the Scripture, the Holy Spirit sends the nourishing sap from the Vine to the branch. For those in Christ, Bible intake is a feast and a privilege. It is the family meal for the adopted sons of God. The Father welcomes us to his table as he welcomes his own Son. And it is at this family table in Christ that we receive blessing and learn to gladly abide in communion with God. Eating the Bible and digesting it through prayer in our identity in Christ is the source of energy that keeps the Great Commission servant persevering in glad-hearted contentment.

But a Bible-less soul is a prayerless soul. And a prayerless soul is a powerless soul. If that describes us, we should not despair. It does not necessarily mean we are dead and apart from Christ. It does not mean God is annoyed and nagging us. God's perfect love is not irritable. The Bible assumes we will need occasional renewal and revival. And Christ is mighty and willing to restore our souls. He will revive us according to his word. So, take, eat, and see that he is good. He will not turn us away, even if we have already skipped a bunch of meals.

We Are What We Eat

We live in a microwave world. Someone may recommend to us the latest clothing item, movie, book, or supplement. Within minutes we can order it on our favorite shopping app. We expect it to be delivered before the end of the week. We spend little time deliberating over these impulsive decisions. But isn't it interesting how powerful just a bit of rumination can be in creating habits, whether they be virtues or vices. Small habits create patterns that cascade into big life changes.

Our biggest decisions and accomplishments in life are carried on the backs of those little decisions and thoughts we chew on when we are not preoccupied with other things. Our daydreams when there are no other competing thoughts tell us about the health of our souls more than nearly anything else. We are what we eat. We morph into our musings. Our integrity in secret thoughts is no different than our integrity in public acts.

We all know that Bible intake is essential for Christian life and growth. Yet, affirming this truth and acting upon it are two different things. We go through seasons of high expectations—recommitting ourselves on the first of January to a new Bible reading plan. Like those who rush to the gym at the beginning of the new year, our spiritual diets start off with enthusiasm and then dissolve when we get to Leviticus.

Most of us undergo self-ridicule because we think we can muscle ourselves into consistent holy habits. We play the comparison game. We reinforce in our imagination that "successful" gospel servants (however we measure success) maintain dutiful times in the word. After all, God reserves his special tasks for his holiest of servants. And Bible intake is the highway to holiness. So we ramp up our resolve. We rededicate once again. Sometimes we entertain an apathetic resignation. We think we just don't have it in us. It's okay, we console ourselves; God doesn't *need* us. Plus, being one of his "great ones" is too much of a burden.

This kind of defeatist mindset is tragic. It is a smack in the face of our vital union with Christ. If we do not remember to rest in our oneness with Christ, we will operate as though our identity rests in our performance. We will treat the Bible as the means to "getting back in" Christ through being filled by the Spirit. We mistakenly think this is the anointing for walking in power. We even act like seers who peer into the secret providences of God and unlock encrypted messages to detect our lack of success.

Too many Great Commission servants start off with dreams and noble goals of doing great things for God, actualizing his promises. Some believe that if we could just catalyze disciple-making movements of obedience-based discipleship, we could finish the Great Commission in our generation. They suggest that finishing the Great Commission is a matter of church-planting methodology—if we could start simple, rapidly reproducing church-planting movements, their groundswell would spill over into all the unreached people groups. Then Jesus would return.

Others assert that we must minimize our doctrinal differences and unite in love for God and one another—then the world would know we are Christians. Still others promote discipling the nation's rulers and powerbrokers of culture, media, and education. Then Christ would return to a Christianized world. Some claim that God is waiting to bless us with his promises if we could just live the Sermon-on-the-Mount lifestyle.

This kind of enthusiasm for innovatively using the Bible to accomplish noble ends never produces a proportionate output. The ordinary realism of slow gospel service deflates our extraordinary idealism. Here's the problem: God's word is not a prop. It is not a means for accomplishing our vision. But we misuse it when we try to make a case for our methods by quoting Scripture.

Taking the Lord's Name and Word in Vain

The examples above illustrate a utilitarian approach to the Bible that all of us probably struggle with at some point in our ministry. I certainly have. And occasionally I still catch myself thinking that way. Turning biblical insights, inferences, and implications into imperatives mangles God's word. The most common example is taking the descriptive passages in Acts and applying them as prescriptive commands for what God expects the church to be like in every age—similar church-planting movements could be ours if and only if we have equal apostolic boldness, doctrinal simplicity, and Spirit-filled power to obey God with total submission.

When we treat the Bible as "useful" or as a "defense" for the tactics we use to fulfill the Great Commission, we are in danger of taking the Lord's name in vain. How so? The way we treat God's word demonstrates how we honor him. Do we trust in, hope in, abide in, and keep his word? Do we hear it but pay no heed? Do we use it to get ministry results? Do we talk about obeying its principles so that we would get more blessings in life? There is a direct connection between our response to God's word and our reverence for God.

For example, in Galatians 3:8, Paul quotes Genesis when God spoke to Abraham, but says the Scripture preached the gospel to Abraham: "And the Scripture, foreseeing that God would justify the gentiles by faith, preached the gospel beforehand to Abraham, saying, 'In you shall all the nations be blessed.'" This is an example of metonymy. It's a literary device that substitutes a word with another word that is very closely identified with it. A common phrase that might help us understand this is, "the pen is mightier than the sword." Pen is a metonymy for the written text, while sword is a metonymy for military power. Similarly, where the Bible speaks, God speaks. If we want to hear the voice of God, read the Bible. The written word *is* the word of God. It neither becomes the word of God, nor does it contain the word of God.

Furthermore, God is equally devoted to his written word as he is to ascribing honor to his own name. The Psalmist says, "I bow down toward your holy temple and give thanks to your name for your steadfast love and your faithfulness, for you have exalted above all things your name and your word" (Ps 138:2). This Hebrew parallelism demonstrates that God exalts his word in the same measure that he exalts his name. Show me a Great Commission servant who reveres and upholds the word of God, and I will show you someone who reveres and upholds the name of God. But show me a Great Commission servant who innovates, reimagines, and merely "utilizes" the word of God, and I will show you someone who should beware lest they take the Lord's name in vain.

The Sufficient and Reliable Word in Christ

One of the challenges in Great Commission service today is not only that there are so many unreached people groups, but that there are so many undiscipled people groups. Many popular statisticians claim these groups are reached simply because some individuals within those groups have indicated an interest in Jesus. An added challenge is that so many missionaries (even Bible translators) have never been tested and proven in their competency in doctrinal, historical, and biblical theology. They often look to strategies and methods for ministry success. Despite their good intentions, they frequently use the Bible like a manual for service rather than a message for salvation.

We claim to believe the Bible is authoritative and sufficient. However, we must press the issue further and ask, sufficient for what? The question is not, is the Bible sufficient and reliable? The question is, *to what end* is the Bible sufficient and reliable? What is the purpose and design of the Bible's sufficiency?

For something to be sufficient or reliable it must perform and produce what it promises. A new car is promised to be reliable and sufficient to take us to the store and back. But a new car is not sufficient or reliable to mow our lawn. A car and a riding lawnmower each have a motor, steering wheel, four wheels, and both go forward and backward. However, their special designs restrict how they perform. Their input determines their output.

What promise does the Bible make for itself? Why is it problematic if we come to the Bible to find out what it can do for us personally, or how it can help our ministry? Doing so indicates a defective view of the Holy Spirit. Too often we treat the Holy Spirit as either a buzz or some sort of crystal ball that can hint at our future or the best path for ministry success. Or even worse, we don't even acknowledge the purpose of the Holy Spirit's inspiration.

If we make the Bible speak where it's silent, then we silence the Bible where it speaks. Too often we force the Bible to speak about everything: church-planting methods, women in ministry, spiritual warfare, culture-making, oppressed vs. oppressor, spiritual leadership, child-rearing, training leaders, obedience-based discipleship, family counseling, healing prayer, etc. When we make imperatives out of its inferences and implications, we have abandoned Scripture's designed purpose. We treat it like it is reliable for something beyond what it promises. There is one primary purpose of the Bible, which all the other secondary and tertiary purposes support: to glorify Jesus Christ and to bring us to Christ and conform us to his image—union and communion with Christ to the glory of the triune God.

Listen to the Witnesses and Look to Jesus

From Genesis to Revelation, the message of Scripture is unashamedly Christ-centered, not Christian-centered. In a pragmatic age, our motto is:

"if it works, then it must be true." We want devotions, Bible studies, and sermons that are useful, relevant, and practical for what we perceive to be our challenges and goals. But we don't need to make the Bible relevant for our lives. We just need to show where the Bible is sufficiently relevant on its own terms. The Bible *is* useful. But useful for what? To what end did the Holy Spirit inspire the Bible? The Bible is sufficient for the purpose of its inspiration—to bear witness to Jesus.

All of the inspired Old Testament Scriptures point to Christ. Paul reminds Timothy that these Scriptures should lead to faith in Christ: "From childhood you have been acquainted with the sacred writings, which are able to make you wise for salvation through faith in Christ Jesus" (2 Tim 3:15; cf. 1 Pet 1:10–11). Jesus himself claimed that the Scriptures testify about him (John 5:39–46). He even scolded his disciples for not knowing such things. He explained to them everything written in the Law of Moses, the Psalms, and the Prophets that pointed to him:

> And beginning with Moses and all the Prophets, he interpreted to them in all the Scriptures the things concerning himself. … Then he said to them, "These are my words that I spoke to you while I was still with you, that everything written about me in the Law of Moses and the Prophets and the Psalms must be fulfilled." Then he opened their minds to understand the Scriptures and said to them, "Thus it is written that the Christ should suffer and on the third day rise from the dead, and that repentance and the forgiveness of sins should be proclaimed in His name to all nations. (Luke 24:27, 44–47)

Isn't it interesting that the Great Commission came soon after these days of sitting under Christ's teaching? This new interpretive paradigm is essential for the establishment and maturity of Great Commission churches throughout the ages. In Matthew 28:18–20 Jesus gives the command to make disciples of all nations by teaching them to keep all that he commanded. Of course, this implies his parables and other teachings from his three years of ministry. But in the local context, he is referring to everything he just unpacked about himself from the Old Testament in Luke 24 and after his resurrection. This is why a "red-letter-Bible" or a pocket New Testament is an imbalanced approach to Scripture. The Old Testament is mainly a Christian book, not primarily a Jewish one.

In Christ, the Old Testament contains our spiritual heritage. It is a stunning gift to draw us closer in communion with him. Moreover, isn't it fascinating that the New Testament believers in Acts used the Old Testament Scriptures for evangelizing (and then discipling) both Jews and gentiles alike (cf. Acts 3:18, 22–24; 10:43; 17:2–3; 26:22–23). Their use of the Old Testament in the early church wasn't merely effective for synagogue-educated Jews. God used the Old Testament Scriptures as revealed in Christ to open the spiritual eyes of the gentiles.

The end goal of the Bible's sufficiency is not to mainly tell us how we should obey. While it does teach us what and how to obey, that is not the main point. Let's say a Jew, Muslim, Buddhist, Hindu, or Mormon were to hear a sermon or a lesson about David and Goliath. And the teacher concluded, "The moral of the story is that you and God can do anything. If you just have faith, you can face any giant. The bigger they come, the harder they fall." Or, let's say the story was about Jacob and Esau, and the theme was "biblical ways to reconcile sibling rivalry." Then let's say the non-Christian visitor were to say afterwards, "that was a really helpful, insightful talk." If that were their response, then that message was not Christian. It was just another practical message that silenced the good news of Jesus Christ. It was not much different than what a Jewish rabbi or some other self-help psychologist might do with the same narrative.

Jesus indeed fulfills explicit prophecies from passages like Psalm 22 about his substitution for us as our Lamb. Further, he fully embodies implicit patterns from passages like Psalm 23 about his service to us as our Shepherd. He fulfills and fills full the pictures and patterns of major characters and major redemptive events of the Old Testament, not necessarily all the little historical details. So, a helpful approach is to observe the big patterns without over analyzing the small pieces. These patterns point us to the Messiah who will be the better expression of those characters and events.

Hebrews 11 is not a list of heroes of the faith; it's a list of failures who had faith. That's why Hebrews 12:1–2 does not tell us to look to the great cloud of witnesses of the Old Testament recorded in Hebrews 11. But look to the one to whom they bear witness: "looking to Jesus, the founder and perfecter of our faith." There is only one hero. He is the hero of every story. The Bible's end goal is to sufficiently point us to look to Jesus.

If we do not rightly handle and keep the word as Jesus commanded, our Great Commission service falls short. It doesn't matter how much time, money, and manpower we invest. In Matthew 28:20, the word *observe*, sometimes translated as *keep*, carries the connotation of a soldier guarding, defending, and watching over his post. It's the same word used a chapter earlier to describe the Roman soldiers keeping watch over Jesus on the cross (Matt 27:36). More than merely suggesting obedience to a set of standards,"keep" calls for a sentinel-like watchfulness over truth. It's a conscription to duty, honor, and fidelity to the word.

The word *disciple* means "apprentice" or "student." So, to be a disciple of Christ means to be a student who, baptized within the context of a local church, studies to show himself approved unto God (2 Tim 2:15). Such a student does this by keeping, guarding, and preserving the word of Christ. The call to biblically discipling the nations emphasizes doctrine-based apologetics and polemics more than obedience-based rule-keeping and habit formation. We must know what we believe and why we believe it. To be sure, new holy habits develop—they must. But the locus of biblical discipleship highlights the supremacy of Christ in all of Scripture and in the life of the believer. It then presses these truths into the mind, rousing the affections, influencing the volition. Faithfulness grows organically out of the soil of nourished gospel faith.

Keeping Christ's Word in Great Commission Spirituality

The ministry organization, the Navigators, has a popular discipleship tool called the Word Hand Illustration.[1] I have used it for many years. A friend introduced it to me back in Bible college as a five-fingered-grip on the word of God. I still use it in my teaching on Bible study methods and spiritual growth principles. Basically, each finger represents one way the Bible prescribes Bible intake, or taking in the word:

- Hearing is the pinkie finger (Rom 10:17)
- Reading is the ring finger (Rev 1:3)
- Studying is the middle finger (Acts 17:11)
- Memorizing is the index finger (Ps 119:9–11)
- Meditation is the thumb (Ps 1:2–3)

1 Navigators, "Word Hand Illustration."

We must hear the word of Christ to receive and grow in faith. We must read the word of Christ to learn its overall content. We must study the word of Christ to understand its literary, theological, doctrinal, and grammatical contexts and boundaries. We must memorize the word of Christ to live in communion with Christ. And we must meditate on the word of Christ to deeply digest and absorb what we have heard, read, studied, and memorized. Meditation is for enjoying the closeness of our union with Christ through Spirit-led communion and conformity to him.

The five-fingered grip represents how we grasp, remember, and keep the word of Christ. It is how we store up the word in our hearts that we might not sin against the Lord (Ps 119:11). Some fingers are stronger than others. But of all the digits on our hand, which one ensures the usefulness of the other four? Which digit would be the most difficult to live without? The thumb, of course. The thumb is the one digit that naturally touches the other four fingers. It is the one digit that completes a fist or clutches onto something. Imagine using chopsticks or a pencil without a thumb. Imagine hanging Christmas ornaments or hanging on the rung of a ladder without a thumb.

Meditation is the most misunderstood and neglected of the five. Lack of biblical meditation probably contributes to our persistent feelings of spiritual exhaustion and waning assurance. It affects our lack of confidence in the Scriptures to convert, comfort, and conform us to Christ. For a disciple to abide in Christ by keeping his word through prayer, the Bible commends biblical meditation. That is precisely what the word *observe* or *keep* in the Great Commission suggests, and exactly how obedient, rabbi-following Jewish apprentices would practice it. A rabbi's student would practice keeping, minding, preserving, and remembering the word. How so? Through meditating on it day and night—abiding, ruminating, chewing on it as daily food.

Avoiding Counterfeit Meditation

Biblical meditation is not the same as popular meditation in yoga, New Age spirituality, medical science, psychiatry, and the like. Biblical meditation commands we fill our minds actively with God's truth. All others require passively emptying our minds. Biblical meditation gives content to chew on. All others call us to visualize and create our own realities. Great Commission spirituality is emphatically not endorsing the emptying of our minds. It does not encourage imaginative prayer or the visualization of God. The Bible forbids any created image of God, including our imaginary ones. It is idolatry (Exod 20:4). Watch out and avoid the popular counterfeits that go beyond what is written in Scripture.

Meditation shouldn't seem so off-limits to us. Yet, many sadly associate it with pagan spirituality. Surprisingly, we all naturally meditate. But most of us don't realize it. For instance, in Psalm 1, the blessed man "meditates day and night." But in Psalm 2, the nations rage against God and "plot in vain." The same Hebrew verb is used for biblical "meditation" in Psalm 1 and vain "plotting" in Psalm 2. The mind, heart, and will are always active.

Habitual sin is essentially misapplied and misdirected meditation. If a person commits adultery, it was because that person let their mind think over and over about someone other than their spouse. After a season of daydreaming about that person without turning away from their fantasies, their desires follow what their mind has been chewing on. Then their wills are compelled to take action based on their desires.

Or, imagine the father who comes home from work, saunters through the door, and kicks his son's toy truck across the room. Everyone freezes and wonders what got into dad. Why is he so mad? Well, dad received a reprimand from his boss for something that was not his fault. He spent the whole day visualizing himself yelling at his boss for such ridiculous accusations. His drive home was fraught with rude drivers, and he had the radio blasting a heated talk-radio program decrying governmental corruption. Dad spent the whole day stewing with angry thoughts. So, when he came home, it only took a small toy truck on the floor to ignite his rage.

If a person struggles with sinful anger, it is because they meditate on whatever makes them angry. If a person struggles with fear or discontentment, it is because they meditate on what is frightening or disagreeable. If a person struggles with sexual bondage, it is because they let lustful thoughts linger and dwell in their mind. And to be clear, struggling with habitual sin and being tempted by sin are two different things. We are all tempted in this world, just as was Christ in his humanity. And sinning, giving into temptation, is still different than living in a pattern of sin.

Habitual sin comes from consistent choices based upon disordered affections. And those inordinate desires grow out of a mind set on the flesh.

Habitual sin is always a meditation fail. Meditation is like magnetism—we get pulled in the direction of our meditation. Our hearts are magnetized to move toward whatever our minds are set on, and we make choices according to the strongest desires of our hearts. As Jonathan Edwards would notably say, we always choose according to our prevailing inclinations, or strongest desires.[2] What we think about the most drives our desires; we become like what we behold.

Reading Aloud and Meditation

There's something physiological about how the brain retains what the eyes read, what the ears hear, and what the mouth and vocal cords utter. In my doctoral studies, I read research that demonstrated that the brain remembers and recalls words better through reading aloud than merely hearing, silently reading, acting, or watching. Developmental psychology suggests that children learn to read best when they read aloud. In fact, before the industrial revolution in the West with all its factory and manufacturing noises, what was the loudest place in any large city? The library. Everyone read aloud in the library. Until the advent of silent reading in Western education of the early nineteenth century, people viewed silent reading as idle and even snobbish. Reading was always a social practice—something from which even bystanders could benefit.

In Jewish tradition, those who had access to copies of the Law would read aloud over and over to themselves in a mumbling sort of way. This was to remember it, meditate on it, and teach it. And those who didn't have access would imitate word-for-word those who had memorized portions. The early Christians in the Latin, Greek, and Celtic churches applied the practice that was likely passed on from the early Jewish Christian leaders. This practice influenced their approach to memorizing the Psalms for discipleship and memorizing the creeds. Such oral meditation practices persisted for the next eighteen hundred years.

Even today in many countries around the world, most people still read aloud to themselves. I remember serving in countries before cell phones were ubiquitous and certainly before smart phones and social media were available. People sat at the bus stops, at their noodle stands, on a park bench, and they read aloud to themselves. They read aloud from books,

2 Edwards, *Works*, Kindle Edition, Location 13427.

the newspaper, or whatever other printed material they had. I rarely saw anyone reading quietly to themselves. Biblical meditation is merely the natural human method of reading aloud but over and over for the sake of recall, memory, and insight. There's nothing mystical or cryptic about it. It's totally normal and natural.

But Christians should not meditate on movie quotes, sports statistics, or political social media outrage. The content of our meditation is a divine book. Though stories might be inspiring, the Bible is the only inspired book. More than being informed or entertained, when we meditate on the Bible, we behold the glory of Christ. It transforms us by degrees into Christ's image.

Meditation Application

Here is where we get pointedly practical. This may be the most practical section in this book. Let's take all the content of this chapter thus far and apply it to one text in a useful way to see how we can meditate on the word of Christ for growing in closeness and conformity to him.

Let's look at Joshua 1:5–9 and listen for how it sufficiently points us to look to Christ and conform to him. This explanation will illustrate what it looks like to meditate on the word of Christ and remain mindful of our vital union with Christ. He has already made us clean. He has already grafted us into all the blessings laid out in this passage since he has fulfilled them in his obedience. We merely respond by faith alone. And we then live in grateful imitation of him.

Here is the historical and literary context: Moses has recently died. He was God's prophet and Law-giver, God's great high priest, God's deliverer of his people from Egypt, a man who spoke with God as a man speaks to his friend, and the most humble man who ever lived.

However, the humblest man that ever lived was forbidden from entering the Promised Land. Why? Numbers 20:9–12 records that God told Moses to speak to the rock so that water would come out. But, in exasperation because of the people's rebellion, Moses instead struck the rock with his staff. Because he disobeyed God's word, he was prohibited from walking into the land of God's blessing. As the leader, Moses had a greater disclosure of God's self-revelation than the rest. With greater disclosure comes greater accountability.

Now Joshua must replace Moses as the leader of approximately two million Hebrews. He must carefully keep God's instructions in order to lead the people into Canaan and conquer its wicked inhabitants. Joshua is not Moses, but he serves the same God, with the same standards. To say the least, Joshua has a demanding, high-stress job. He must lead millions of men, women, and children who have no land or houses of their own. They are discontent with the meagerness of their food and the years of wandering. They are a wearisome people, always grumbling, quarrelling, and complaining. They are easily frightened by the challenges and hardships ahead of them. And worst of all, they all are quick to forget God. They will not and cannot keep his Law. If they do not meditate on God's Law, they will not keep it; and if they do not keep it, they will be fearful and not experience the blessing of God's abiding presence in taking the land.

Especially for those in ministry or leadership, Joshua 1:5–9 is quite familiar. Yet familiarity with parts of the Bible can create indifference and idleness. We tend to skim over such passage as though we were scanning through an old issue of a magazine.

Identifying the main burden of this passage does not require a commentary or knowledge of Hebrew. Just read through these verses over and over. Look at them carefully. Look into them reflectively. Write down any observation. Basic sentence diagramming can be more helpful than most in-depth historical background commentaries. Since this passage is one of the key texts in the Bible on meditation, I am going to unpack it to teach about the *value* of meditation. Then I'll diagram it to teach the *process* of meditation.

One main observation is that the structure of this text is essential for understanding the main point. In the Old Testament especially, the patterns and structures of sentences and content significantly influence the main points. Here is a simplified outline of the sentence structure:

(5b) I will be with you
  (6, 7a) Be strong and courageous;
    (7b) being careful to do according to all the law
      (7d) that you might have good success
        (8a) This Book of the Law shall not depart from your mouth;
        (8b) but you shall meditate on it day and night
      (8c) so that you may be careful to do according to do all that is written in it
    (8e) and then you will have good success
  (9a) be strong and courageous
(9b) the LORD your God is with you

This is a chiastic structure, which is quite common particularly in the Old Testament for making a strong literary and theological point. This is true at both the micro-level within paragraphs and macro-level within books. A chiasm looks like half of an 'X.' For example:

A
  B
    C
    CC
  BB
AA

Typically, the most important part is the center parallel sentences (C and CC). And the second most important part is the first and last parallel verses (A and AA). By meditating and simply noticing the repetition of ideas in the text, the priorities of God's message in this passage become clear. Here are some easy observations:

First, let's remember to read it as Spirit-filled Christians and not Jews. God promises his abiding presence, which is the foundation of our motivation for meditation. We can meditate not because we *hope* God will be there, but because we *know* he is there. Always. In Christ, he is not only always with us, but he is in us. His life is vitally our life, sourcing us, serving us, and strengthening us. Those who are adopted into the family of God and united with Christ can never leave the Father's presence. He is always there waiting for his children to listen to him, obey him, and enjoy their union with Christ. Therefore, God's enduring presence in Christ is the foundation of meditation.

Next, we should consider the commands to be courageous—very courageous. Why? Because we are easily frightened and disheartened. What would it look like to live lives of courage? It looks like keeping God's word. How much of the word? The whole counsel of God.

What is the fruit of courageously keeping God's word? Good success. The term *success* in our generation has been marketed by self-help psychology and secular leadership terminology. Since that is the case, we must find out what success means biblically. Essentially, biblical success is acting wisely, living in the fear of God and enjoying his favor, thriving in the pleasure of God's good grace, and enjoying the benefits and blessings of being among the faithful. The Hebrew word for *success* or *prosper* can be used to refer to a vine that thrives (Ezek 17:9) or a weapon that prevails (Isa 54:17).

In other words, biblical prosperity and success look like something flourishing according to its intended design. The foundation of meditation is that God is with us in Christ. The blessing of meditation is enjoying his already abiding presence in closeness and conformity to him. This is spiritual prosperity and acting wisely. This is how God designed us to be in Christ.

And now, where do we get the courage to keep the word in order to enjoy the blessing of the Lord's presence? Biblical meditation. This is the most important point in the passage. How do we know? Look at how this passage highlights it. Notice there are two commands in verse 8. There is a negative command: "don't let the words of this book depart from your mouth." And there is a positive command: "meditate on it day and night."

Clearly, there is a relationship between meditation and what we do with our mouth. The Bible says "out of the abundance of the heart, the mouth speaks" (Matt 12:34); and "let the words of my mouth and the meditation of my heart be acceptable in your sight" (Ps 19:14). And the word for *meditate* means to "mumble repetitively" and to "chew on," like a cow chews its cud. Meditation is keeping the food of the word from leaving our mouths.

Meditation Practice

One way to meditate is by handwriting the verse or verses over and over and circling words or phrases that seem most wonderful and applicable. But there is another simple way of meditating on a verse. It corresponds more closely to the ancient Hebrew and ancient Christian practices: read a verse or two aloud over and over to yourself. Each time you repeat it, emphasize the next main word or part in the order of the verse.

For example: "*This* Book of the Law shall not depart from your mouth. This *Book* of the Law shall not depart from your mouth. This Book of the *Law* shall not depart from your mouth. This Book of the Law *shall not* depart from your mouth. This Book of the Law shall not *depart* from your mouth. This Book of the Law shall not depart from *your mouth*."

Do this until you have made it through the verse or section entirely. Each time, try emphasizing something different. Accentuate the subject, the verb, the object, the preposition, the logical connector. You don't have to do it loudly. Just do it under your breath. Consider how the Holy Spirit inspired each word. Think of its significance over against another word. For example, why a "book" and not merely a story, image, or picture? And why *this* book as opposed to other books? What does the verb *depart* imply? Why use *mouth* instead of heart or mind? How does not letting the book slip out of your mouth relate to meditation in the next clause? Why so frequent? Why so careful?

Try it now with Joshua 1:8. Read it over and over. Each time put stress on a new word: *Book, Law, depart, mouth, but, meditate, day and night, so that, careful, do, all, written.* After emphasizing a new word or phrase, ruminate on why that word is significant. Why did the Holy Spirit choose that word? How does that sentence relate to the sentence before and after it? If that word or sentence disappeared from our Bibles, what amount of spiritual gold would we be missing? If that verse departed from our mind, what nourishing food would we lack? Would we feel hungry? Would we be desperate to find it?

God says that "man does not live by bread alone; but man lives by every word that comes from the mouth of the LORD" (Deut 8:3). Meditation is chewing on, eating, and digesting the word of God. When we are surrounded by famished and starving people, the evidence that we are prosperous and thriving is that we are chewing and feasting on good food day and night. Our hunger is being satisfied. Our strength is renewed every day.

My former PhD professor, Don Whitney, would often say that Bible reading is exposure to Scripture. And meditation is the absorption of Scripture.[3] He would suggest that if we are so busy that we only have ten minutes to be with the Lord in a day, we should spend the first two minutes

3 For a helpful chapter on biblical meditation, see Whitney, *Spiritual Disciplines*, 41–64. I am grateful to Dr. Whitney who influenced me in much of what I know and teach about biblical meditation.

reading, the next five minutes meditating on a select portion of what we just read, followed by three minutes praying through our meditation. That ten-minute breakdown demonstrates the priority of meditation within Bible intake and prayer.

Bible reading without meditation is like dipping a tea bag into hot water for one second. The hot water was only exposed briefly to the tea bag. But there is not much evidence at all that the tea bag ever entered the water. And the tea bag certainly didn't affect the water. However, when we let the tea bag soak in the water for a few minutes, the tea colors and flavors the water. The water transforms with new properties. It is no longer water. It is tea. The design of the tea has conformed the water to itself through a vital diffusion of the tea's essence.[4]

We must avoid simply settling for a brief exposure to Scripture. Instead, it would be wise to plan a place and time to absorb Scripture through meditation. Even if it is only five minutes. God's word colors and flavors our worldview, our thinking, our affections, and our wills. The Puritan pastor, Thomas Watson, said: "The reason we come away so cold from reading the word is, because we do not warm ourselves at the fire of meditation."[5] Whitney puts it clearly: "As the fire blazes more brightly and clearly, it gives off more light (insight and understanding) and heat (passion for obedient action). 'Then,' says the Lord, 'you will be prosperous and successful.'"[6]

Noticing the Context of Christ's Word

The main application point of this passage in Joshua is that biblical meditation leads us to courageously keep the Scripture. As a result, we enjoy flourishing in God's presence. The converse is also true: unbiblical meditation diverts us from Scripture into fearful disobedience. As a consequence, we languish without the enjoyment of God's sweet presence. If we persist without turning back, God may use his fatherly discipline to snatch us back.

However, we must be careful to avoid a pre-Christian, law-based, synagogue devotional that neglects God's grace. Let's remember that the Bible is Christ-centered and not Christian-centered. So, how do we meditate Christianly? How do we meditate and remain mindful of our union with

4 Whitney, *Spiritual Disciplines*, 48.

5 Whitney, 49.

6 Whitney, 49.

Christ? To answer these questions, let's begin by considering whether we are in Joshua's shoes or Jesus's shadow. In other words, is this something for us to fulfill like the Old Testament Joshua? Or is this something that has been fulfilled for us by the New Testament Yeshua? To rightly get at the context in Christ, we must meditate on what the passage teaches us about God, Man, Christ, and our reasonable response in Christ.

God

What does this passage show us about God? It teaches us that God will never leave us. That he has spoken to us. That he expects us to keep his word. And that he has a desire for our spiritual flourishing. But that flourishing can only come about through a very specific means: courageously keeping the word through meditating on the word of God.

Man

How does this passage portray man? In Adam's corruption, we are all easily frightened and disheartened. We are prone to wander from God and to forget God's word. Yet, God loves mankind and wants what is good and best according to why he made us—to walk with him in love and thrive in his ways.

Christ

How does this passage set us up to look to Christ and respond as Christians? Better yet, more poignant questions would be: Whom is the spirit of Christ through Joshua telling us to consider? What is the Christ-centered instinct we can sense in this passage? In what ways might this passage prompt us to hope in a better Prophet, Priest, or King?

Response

Is this passage intended to teach us to emulate Joshua's courageous leadership techniques? God's standards of obedience for leadership success? Or to focus our worship on the one to whom Joshua points? To be sure, there are moral and practical lessons in this passage. But they are all driving at something, or someone, infinitely more worthy of our imitation.

Jesus (Yeshua) is the better Joshua who meditated on the Law of the Lord both day and night. He perfectly kept all that was written in it. "The will of the LORD shall prosper in his hand" (Isa 53:10). He fulfilled perfectly what Joshua should have done. He filled full the pattern of Joshua's calling and leadership. He entered the Jordan River and defeated his enemies on the mount. He leads God's people to the land of God's promised blessing and rest. And in union with this divine Joshua, we respond by meditating on his law of peace—the gospel. Our courage and success in Christ are not our own. We are victorious because the victorious Yeshua is our life.

A Prayerful Instinct of Abiding in the Word of Christ

The steely resolve in Great Commission service to take Christ's good news to the outposts of the empire and risk our lives for his honor comes from abiding in his word. Abiding in Christ by biblical meditation through prayer is truly the practical rhythm of Great Commission spirituality. The word of Christ gives us faith and strength (cf. Rom 10:17; 16:25) to labor in him. The Bible is not finally about what we must do as much as it is about what Christ has done and who he is. In light of that truth, we meditate on the word as it leads us to trust in Christ as our Prophet, Priest, and King. Then, and only then, do we have the boldness of Christ to serve the unreached and undiscipled peoples. Such otherworldly courage can only be explained by the power of Christ in us.

Do you remember what the disciples said after Jesus showed them how he fulfills all the Old Testament Scriptures? "They said to each other, 'Did not our hearts burn within us while he talked to us on the road, while he opened to us the Scriptures?'" (Luke 24:32). When Great Commission servants meditate on the word of Christ this way, it rejoices the heart, enlightens the eyes, makes wise the simple, and revives the soul (Ps 19:7–8). Our hearts will burn within us as we meditate on the word of Christ. God will grant us courage to keep—guard, treasure, observe, defend—all that is written in it.

> *As the outward man is not fit for work for any length of time unless he eats, so it is with the inner man. What is the food for the inner man? Not prayer, but the Word of God—not the simple reading of the Word of God, so that it only passes through our minds, just as water runs through a pipe. No, we must consider what we read, ponder over it, and apply it to our hearts.*
>
> —George Müller

Chapter 4 Contemplation

Abiding in Christ within God's World

Scripture for Meditation

> Set your minds on things that are above, not on things that are on earth. For you have died, and your life is hidden with Christ in God. When Christ who is your life appears, then you also will appear with him in glory.
>
> —Colossians 3:2–4

My grandfather controlled the room. He was the thermostat that set the temperature. But his temperature was neither too hot, nor too cold. I have no memory of ever feeling chilly around him. No one felt shut down by unfriendliness or aloofness. Neither do I remember feeling hot with anger around him, turned up by irritability or nitpickiness. No, my grandfather knew how to make people laugh at his tall tales. He made everyone feel relaxed like everything was okay.

He exuded a recreational spirit. He could sit quietly in his chair in the shade. He could marvel like a child at a hummingbird. He could enthusiastically throw a slobbery ball for his border collie. Or he could take a morning walk down his street and each time notice something fascinating in the trees and mountains. He always seemed so charmed and childlike with his curious eye. He was a retired university professor, and his leisurely spirit took joy in the fruit of his life. He had the mind of a scholar and the heart of a school boy. In retirement, his work was finished. Whenever he was around, all was well. All was captivating. I felt at rest. I felt at home.

Learning to Look

From a young age, sages like my grandfather, mother, and father influenced me to value rest and leisure in God's good providences. I learned to listen to creation as a symphonic movement composed by a master musician. I learned how to view God's common graces as windows into heavenly realities. They were not mirrors of my self-worth. Neither were they portraits hung as decorations to be glanced at occasionally. I learned to not merely look *at* God's word and God's world. The eyes of my heart learned to look *into* God's word and God's world. I learned to look for God's fingerprints of providence in everything.

I learned to see creation how Alan Jacobs memorably described C. S. Lewis's childlike wonder at the ordinary bits of creation—the wetness of water, the scent of leather, the camouflage of a chameleon, the whistling wind through the pines. Jacobs described Lewis's mind as "above all characterized by a *willingness to be enchanted* … [e.g.,] his delight in laughter, his willingness to accept a world made by a good and loving God, and (in some ways above all) his willingness to submit to the charms of a wonderful *story*."[1] Jacobs beautifully dubbed Lewis's Christian enthrallment in God's wonderful world an "omnivorous attentiveness."[2]

As the Puritan, Richard Sibbes, would put it, "The whole life of a Christian should be nothing but praises and thanks to God. We should neither eat, nor drink, nor sleep, but eat to God, and sleep to God, and work to God, and talk to God; do all to his glory and praise."[3]

Another Puritan, John Flavel, would sweetly ruminate on how creation is "altogether lovely" when we see its source and purpose in Christ: "Christ is the very essence of all delights and pleasures, the very soul and substance

---

1 Jacobs, *Narnian*, Kindle Edition, Location 318. Emphasis in original. See also Dorsett, *Seeking the Secret Place*.

2 Jacobs, Location 312.

3 Grosart, *Complete Works*, Kindle Edition, Locations 4694–95.

of them. As all the rivers are gathered into the ocean, which is the meeting-place of all the waters in the world, so Christ is that ocean in which all true delights and pleasures meet. ... There is nothing lovely without him."[4]

From the outset, I should clarify that what I mean by contemplation is seeing in creation and in life those insights and promises that echo Scripture. We must learn to see those patterns, designs, and reasonable deductions that God has deeply imbedded in the created order. Bible-filled saints recognize these universal principles in nature that correspond to what the Bible teaches.

I am not talking about the popular mystical practices of listening for specific prophetic words, impressions, visualizations, or promptings that only make sense to the recipient. I'm not promoting listening for Jesus calling or prophetic whispers about the next steps we're supposed to take in life. I'm simply underscoring our God-given instinct to contemplate all of creation as a reminder to us about its Creator.

I've learned that conforming ourselves to God and learning to see how he sees is crucial for the Great Commission servant. It refreshes those laboring on the frontlines, amidst cold silence, unending dark, and mysterious providences. Great Commission spirituality reminds the gospel servant to stay the course and remain faithful. Why? Because Jesus stands by us. His life is in us, and we are in him. When we look hard enough, we will see evidence of his providence working for us. Sweetness and sovereignty, always and everywhere.

Viewing creation as image-bearers helps the Great Commission servant find joy and hope in the mundane and tedious things. Sibbes put it succinctly: "The life of a Christian is wondrously ruled in this world by the consideration and meditation of the life of another world. Nothing more steers the life of a Christian here than the consideration of the life hereafter."[5]

Consider the odious smells of a pig farm. Only through death, butchering, and an oven's intense heat can the aroma of a ham bring joy to a family holiday. Consider how death and heat can transform a vile pig into mouth-watering bacon. What is God's creation telling us about death, life, transformation, and joy? Much of his creation is a living metaphor for

---

4 Flavel, *Major Works*, 437–38, Kindle Edition, Locations 8445–51.

5 Grosart, *Complete Works*, Kindle Edition, Locations 5701–03.

the saints, an analogy of life. Creation displays God's wise, sovereign, and benevolent providences for us. It is a song with layers of nuance, rhyme, meter, harmonies, dynamic changes, and percussive rhythms.

Each layer deeply affects the saint who knows how to listen. Many hear. But few listen. When all comforts and conveniences are stripped away, Great Commission servants can look into the ordinary and see the extraordinary. These providences remind us: God is there. He is with us, in us, and for us.

Looking to See

Creation is more than meets the eye. Great Commission spirituality invites us to have omnivorous attentiveness to see into God's good designs. Some of us feel like we are suffocating under the pressure of serving in a foreign context. Others are weary of trying to reach and teach hard-hearted people. Some tiptoe around the scrutiny of hyper-surveilling totalitarian governments, while others live amidst fearful villagers haunted by demons. We desperately need an air supply. Pure air. Zion's air.

Great Commission spirituality reminds us: "But ask the beasts, and they will teach you; the birds of the heavens, and they will tell you; or the bushes of the earth, and they will teach you; and the fish of the sea will declare to you" (Job 12:7–8). And, "the heavens declare the glory of God and the sky above proclaims his handiwork. Day to day pours out speech, and night to night reveals knowledge" (Ps 19:1–2). Look. Listen. And live another day in Christ's commission.

This holy habit of contemplating God's lavish kindness in all his world, works, and ways has stopped me from viewing the ordinary as ordinary. Because God wills it and works it for his delight, the ordinary is extraordinary. Under the curse, the ordinariness of creation can seem dull and dour. But looking through the lens of the resurrection and the redeeming work of Christ, we can see and hear truly for the first time. We can learn to see into normal things with an artist's eye and glimpse something of God's good design. We can learn to love people by not just looking at them. We can love them by looking into them. Seeing them.

For example, there's that frowning man at the immigration office who wields so much power over your family's visas in his country. Or the haggard woman who, with a stroke of the pen, determines the adoption status of that special-needs orphan you genuinely desire to add to your family. We can choose to look past their intimidating demeanor and ignore them. Or we can look *into* their scowl lines and wonder what their home life is like. What makes them sad? What makes them laugh? Have they ever met a Christian? Have they even heard of Jesus before? Once we've normalized their common humanity, we can ask the Lord for eyes to see them. Eyes of compassion and hope—compassion for their corruption and condemnation in Adam, and hope that our good God would transform them into a new creation in Christ. This is how Great Commission spirituality helps us see. Instead of seeing old, cracked glass, we look harder and see how the Lord can remake them into stained glass windows.

To be sure, our seeing and hearing are by faith. They are only partial in this life. Although we look through a glass dimly, we still can look. To stay the course in Great Commission service, we must look through all of God's works and world as dim windows into Zion. Great Commission spirituality reframes and recasts the mysterious providences of this life. They become extraordinary-ordinary. Such a God-captivated vision of life becomes less about achieving and more about receiving. This is not a lazy rest—it is a leisurely rest. A Sabbath rest. Jesus said, "It is finished!" He worked for us. And now we enjoy the fruits of his retirement, as it were.

Great Commission spirituality calls us to follow the Lamb wherever he goes, and to follow with glad-hearted contentment and confidence. Why? Because the Lamb shall be exalted in all the nations. It is a promise that he himself shall fulfill. God fulfilled his messianic promises to Abraham through weak strugglers who carried the seed by faith. Likewise, he will fulfill his promise to give Christ the nations as his final inheritance. Great Commission servants are part of the fulfillment of that promise since we are united with Christ.

Moreover, since we are commissioned by Christ, we are participants in him as the promise progressively comes to pass among the unreached. We work in light of his promise, not because he is waiting for us to fulfill it. His Great Commission is not great because it is such a massive imperative. Instead, it is great because it is secured by such magisterial indicatives: "You *will receive* power when the Holy Spirit has come upon you, and you *will be* my witnesses" (Acts 1:8); "*All authority* in heaven and on earth has been *given to me*" (Matt 28:18); and "Behold, *I am with you always*, to the end of the age" (Matt 28:20, emphasis added). Let us, then, strive to enter his rest, while laboring in his vineyard. In him, all is well, and all shall be well.

With an eye to look for the remarkable in the normal, the extraordinary in the ordinary, God opened my eyes. At a young age I was born again. I was spiritually blind, but God made me see. I learned to look into the word and see God's incarnate Word. And then seeing the world through the written word of Christ changed everything. Because of seeing the truth in the word, everything good in the world became beautiful.

It is lovely because Jesus holds it all together by the word of his power. He has supremacy over all that is. This assurance in the sovereignty of Christ bestows peace upon anxious, exhausted Great Commission servants. Before new birth, God's world is intriguing. It's the craft of a genius. After new birth, God's world is beautiful. It's the gift of a good Father. Great Commission spirituality sees the light dawning in the darkness of this world and plods on another day, in hope of the glory of God filling the earth.

Looking through Remembering

As a Great Commission servant, one of the best disciplines to cultivate is remembrance. That's an odd sounding discipline, especially since so many publications focus on practicing holy habits and cultivating more life-giving practices. But remembering implies slowness and stillness. It forces us to revisit those places in our souls and lives that might be less than hospitable. Who actually wants to relive those memories? They might not even be traumatic or scary as much as they are disappointing or maddening. Disappointing because of what they never produced in our lives. And maddening because we threw all our weight into something that God seemed to shut down without explanation. Isn't it strange that we think God owes us detailed reasons for every painful providence he sends into our lives?

Hebrew scholars commonly say that in the Hebrew Bible, the first five books of Moses (the Pentateuch or the Torah) claim the most sacred place in the Hebrew mind. And if there is one book among the five that dominates a Hebrew's affections, the book of Deuteronomy would be the holy of holies. The book of Deuteronomy ties up all the introductory themes and motifs of the Pentateuch and sets up the rest of the Old Testament, passing on those literary and theological themes.

It's helpful to pay attention to the proportionality of emphasis in a book. Take note of a theme or command that the author most often repeats, whether directly or indirectly. If we count God's commands in Deuteronomy and combine topically synonymous imperatives, one of the most frequently uttered commands is to *remember* or *do not forget.* Of course, there are commands for obedience and love, but the command to remember God's works and God's words takes up a curious amount of ink on the pages of Deuteronomy.

Consider one example of the small command to actively remember. Notice how it produces two things. This passage from Deuteronomy 7 will be applied here in principle for the context of a Great Commission servant:

> If you say in your heart, "These nations are greater than I. How can I dispossess them?" *you shall not be afraid of them* but *you shall remember* what the LORD your God did to Pharaoh and to all Egypt, the great trials that your eyes saw, the signs, the wonders, the mighty hand, and the outstretched arm, by which the LORD your God brought you out. So will the LORD your God do to all the peoples of whom you are afraid. … *You shall not be in dread of them, for the LORD your God is in your midst, a great and awesome God.* … And you shall not bring an abominable thing into your house and become devoted to destruction like it. *You shall utterly detest and abhor it, for it is devoted to destruction.* (Deut 7:17–19, 21, 26; emphasis added)

What is the outcome of remembering and recounting the works of God in our life, in the two-thousand-year history of the gospel's triumph around the world, and in the overall redemptive storyline of Scripture? The discipline of remembering God's works, according to this text, serves us in two main ways: We see that remembering God's word and works provides *courage* and *consecration.* Courage: we have no need to fear because God is our Deliverer. Consecration: we should respond to this God with holy devotion, fleeing the values and belief systems of the world.

Remembering for Courage and Consecration

When we stare idly at the global landscape of Bibleless languages—thousands of language groups without even a word for *Jesus*—we feel helpless and hopeless. We can't make even a dent in the task at hand.

The weight of both temporal and eternal needs around the world is utterly jaw-dropping. But we must practice remembering the mighty acts of God in church history. We must remember that God has always worked in the face of seemingly impossible challenges with terribly inadequate servants. This practice gives us comfort in God's goodness to save even us, to save the most resistant peoples, and to use us for his Great Commission purposes.

Remembering that God has used those salty and unsavory Great Commission servants of old, we take courage that God will also abide with undeserving sinners like us. This courage gives us strength to renew our devotion to his word and his commands. The power is in his word, not us. Remembering his word and his works gives us courage to say and do all that the word says, and the humility to say and do no more.

Whether God chooses to save by many or by few, God alone is the one who saves. Who are we to argue with absolute sovereignty? God can do whatever he pleases. And if it pleases God to use us, then he will, in spite of us, every time. David sang, "Remember the wondrous works that he has done, his miracles, and the judgments he uttered" (Ps 105:5). David commended remembering God's faithfulness, though he could have surely wallowed in memories of his own unfaithfulness and his consequently broken family and fractured kingdom.

And just in case we fail to remember and slip back into unfaithfulness, like those before (Ps 78:39–42), David recalls that God himself "remembers his covenant forever, the word that he commanded, for a thousand generations" (Ps 105:8). What is that covenant? The Mosaic Law? Stipulations for blessings or cursing? No. God is remembering his covenant to bless the nations through the Seed of Abraham: "the covenant that he made with Abraham" (Ps 105:9). The Psalms teach us that God remembers his promises to save the nations through the promised Seed of Abraham (Gal 3:16), the Christ (Ps 98:2–3). And all those among the nations who trust in Christ are united to Christ and receive his blessings: "There is neither Jew nor Greek, there is neither slave nor free, there is no male and female, for you are all one in Christ Jesus. And if you are Christ's, then you are Abraham's offspring, heirs according to promise" (Gal 3:28–29).

Essentially, David's song is our song: *Remember.* Remember what? Should we remember our works for God? Should we remember them to keep track of how God will reward us? No. Remember the works of God. God is our great reward.

Should we remember our words to God? Should we remember how we have sought to impress God in the past by our vows of surrender and extravagant dedications? No. Remember the words of God. And above all, we must, "Remember Jesus Christ, risen from the dead, the offspring of David" (2 Tim 2:8). If we are going to actively remember anything, let it be the man seated at God's right hand. Remember him. Remember the Savior-King. Remember who has authority over all creation and eternity and holds all things together by the word of his power. We should contemplate our life *in Christ*. All our memories, experiences, and plans make sense only *in* him.

Contemplating Others as Family in Christ

Great Commission servants are some of the most determined and disciplined Christians. They regularly must choose self-denial and sacrifice to live in harsh environments to serve hard people. Regular self-denial is required for learning a difficult language in order to communicate the gospel. Such servants can have strong personalities at times. A mix of strong-willed temperaments can create friction. This happens even with local believers who do not share the same cultural background and perspectives.

To persevere in love for one another, outdoing one another in showing honor, requires a conscious decision to see one another in Christ. Our new resurrected life in Christ should transform how we see our family, co-workers, and fellow Christians in general.

Consider how Christ's resurrection immediately recast his relationship to his disciples and their relationship to one another. In the garden when Mary Magdelene stumbled upon the risen Christ, notice what he said to her in John 20:17: "Do not cling me, for I have not yet ascended to the Father." Jesus is basically saying, "The time for me to come and stay on earth forever has not come yet. Instead of trying to hold onto me, Mary, I have a job for you." In the text, Jesus told her: "Go to my brothers and say to them, 'I am ascending to my Father and your Father, to my God and your God.'" This is where biblical meditation helps serve our contemplation. What is Jesus saying? Jesus's resurrection has just revolutionized four different relationships.

Our God

Jesus tells Mary to refer to God in the presence of the disciples as "your God." This is not twenty-first century pluralism where everyone has their own god. These words have history. Upon delivering Israel out of slavery in Egypt, God cut a covenantal relationship with them. As with wedding vows, God swore: "I ... will be your God and you shall be my people" (Lev 26:12). This phrasing expresses the heart of covenant: belonging to one another—I belong to you, and you belong to me. Bound together, forever. And in the New Covenant, since death has been destroyed, death will never separate and break our bond.

The disciples would have heard this as an announcement that God inaugurated a new covenantal relationship through a better exodus. God has delivered each of us from slavery to sin and the devil. He did this by means of the death, burial, and resurrection of the better Moses. God and those in Christ now belong together forever. When we look into the unimpressive, broken lives of our fellow gospel servants, let us remember who has delivered them from the bondage of sin that we too were once under.

Our Father

But God is more than just our God. Jesus adds the words, "And your Father." Before Christ's ministry, it was nearly inconceivable for someone to refer to God as Father. Only delusional people could claim such a closeness and familial intimacy with Adonai. It's true that Adam, Israel, and some kings like David are referred to as God's sons, but they all fail miserably. Then the only begotten Son arrives in Bethlehem after four hundred years of silence from the prophets.

He is the true, supreme Son. The Father himself commends Jesus as his beloved Son. In this Son, the Father is well pleased. When we receive this divine Savior-King by virtue of his obedience in life and in death, the Father adopts us into his family. He makes us co-heirs with the Son. This is the heartbeat of Christianity: God is ours, and he is our Father, not merely our Creator or Sovereign. This is the dearest of blessings secured by the resurrection.

The Bible says that Jesus died to bring us to God (1 Pet 3:18). We abide in our Father's house not merely as servants and slaves, but as sons.

We don't merely visit as casual acquaintances, but dwell with full rights and privileges as sons. The Bible emphasizes that we are all (male or female) adopted *sons*—not children. In the biblical cultures sons, not daughters, were the exclusive inheritors and recipients of all the rights and privileges of the father's honor. When we look into the hollow, depressed eyes of our fellow servants, let's remember whom they call Father, just like us. We have the same inheritance in Christ. We have royal blood.

Our Brother

If God is our Father, and Jesus is God's Son, what does this suggest about our relationship to Jesus? He is our King, to be sure. But there is more. He is our Lord certainly. But there is more. He is our Savior, of course. But there is more.

Just as God is not merely our Savior-God, but our Father, Jesus is not merely our Savior-King, but something much more relational and familial. He says it straightaway to Mary in John 20:17, "Go instead to my brothers." Brothers? Those gutless phonies who couldn't even stay awake and pray with him in Gethsemane during Jesus's darkest night? Peter who denied Christ not once, not twice, but three times?

Throughout the Gospels, Jesus only referred to them as servants, disciples, and then just a few days prior he called them "friends." But brothers? He could have scolded them and used their unfaithfulness as a teaching opportunity: "I called you friends when you vowed to be faithful and loyal. But since you betrayed me when I wanted your allegiance the most, I'm going to treat you as servants. You blew your chance. You need to at least rededicate yourselves and surrender all to me." No, Jesus didn't humiliate or castigate them for one second. His affection for his servants and friends is brimming over with mercy. Where their sin increased, his grace increased much more. Jesus refers to his fallen, faithless followers as brothers.

Moreover, those of us in Christ who serve in the Great Commission need to hear again and again that God is our Father and Jesus is our brother. In Christ, God is not ashamed of us. Though we sin in shameful ways, the stains don't stick. There are no blemished sheep in the Shepherd's fold. As Charles Spurgeon reminds us with such soothing words, "You may fear that the Lord has passed you by, but it is not so: he who counts the stars, and calls them by their names, is in no danger of forgetting his own children. He knows your case as thoroughly as if you were the only creature he ever made, or the only saint he ever loved. Approach him and be at peace."[6]

Next time we are faced with a hardened fellow servant, we should look *into* their frown lines of regret, disappointment, and shame. We don't need to know the details. Jesus knows. And they are as safe in Jesus's brotherly affection as we are. Remember they are brothers with us—royalty and beloved in Christ.

Our Family

Since we are raised with Christ in the resurrection, we have him as our brother and God as our Father. Moreover, we have all Christ's other brothers as our family. All worldly emphases on ethnicity, culture, nationality, economic bracket, and skin color are inconsequential to our oneness in Christ. They are important, but not ultimate. We are united together in Christ alone, not in an affinity or celebration of diversity.

Man puts value on skin color, good looks, ability, ethnicity, dress, sex, hygiene, and "outward appearance and not about what is in the heart" (2 Cor 5:12). But thanks be to God, who fondly looks at the heart. Regardless of how we see one another, he sees adopted royal sons, brothers of Christ.

> For as many of you as were baptized into Christ have put on Christ. There is neither Jew nor Greek, there is neither slave nor free, there is no male and female, for you are all one in Christ Jesus. And if you are Christ's, then you are Abraham's offspring, heirs according to promise. (Gal 3:27–29)

Our bloodline in Christ transcends and redefines all other earthly, biological, or ethnic relationships. It doesn't obliterate those temporal relationships—it reorders them under his lordship. Consider the truth that as Christians, we are truer brothers and sisters with one another than we ever will be with our unbelieving family members. Contemplate the identities of those believers who are in our biological families. We are first their brothers. Our Christian spouse, Christian parents, and Christian children are our brothers in Christ before they are our spouse, parents, or children. They are fellow adopted sons of the Father.

6 Spurgeon, *Morning and Evening*, 225.

The resurrection of Christ turned the biological family, with all its temporal loyalties, on its head. Jesus cautioned:

> Do not think that I have come to bring peace to earth. I have not come to bring peace, but a sword. For I have come to set a man against his father, and a daughter against her mother, and a daughter-in-law against her mother-in-law. And a person's enemies will be those of his own household. Whoever loves father or mother more than me is not worthy of me, and whoever loves son or daughter more than me is not worthy of me. (Matt 10:34–37)

Great Commission spirituality contemplates our identity in Christ as individuals and as a Christian family in relationship to one another in Christ. This practice of contemplating our identity together in union with Christ helps create familial camaraderie for Great Commission servants. This spirit of brotherhood is especially sweet when we are separated from biological family by great distances and/or divisive biblical convictions. It also helps us grow in fellowship with those local believers with whom we have no cultural or ethnic commonalities or affinity. Our point of unity and familial warmth is our shared union with Christ. They are our true family. God loves each of his adopted sons as though there were only one of us. Let us contemplate one another as we are—brothers in Christ.

A Prayerful Instinct of Contemplating Life in Christ

My long-term endurance as a Great Commission servant improved gradually as I practiced setting my mind on things above, not on things below. If I did consider things below, I tried to stop looking at them like a naturalist, materialist, or a deist saying, "I caught seven trout this morning," or "the sun rose at 6:00 am," or "I got a parasite," or "the snowstorm shut down the whole city."

Instead, I practiced looking *into* them as under the design and command of Christ. Since my life is hidden with Christ in God, nothing in this life is ultimately bad, coincidental, or random. It's all on purpose. God's good purpose. So, seeing all of life through a God-absorbed vision, I began to stop mid-sentence and correct myself. I would then say instead, "God sent me seven trout to catch this morning," or "God made the sun rise at 6:00 am," or "God ordained a parasite for me," or "God made it snow and shut down the whole city."

Similar to the quotation from Thomas Watson about biblical meditation in the previous chapter, Watson also sweetly commends biblical contemplation of God in all of life and creation as a daily means for rousing our love for him:

> Thinking on God, is an admirable means to increase our LOVE to God. As it was with David's meditations, "As I was musing the fire burned" (Psalm 39:3); so it is with our musing on the Deity. While we are thinking on God—our hearts will kindle in love to him. The reason our affections are so chilled and cold in religion—is that we do not warm them with thoughts of God. … Thinking on God, will by degrees transform us into his image. … By contemplating God's holiness, we are in some measure changed into his likeness! "Beholding as in a mirror the glory of the Lord—we are changed into the same image" (2 Cor. 3:18). The contemplative sight of God was transforming; they had some print of God's holiness upon them; as Moses when he had been on the mount with God, his face shone! (Exod. 34:35). What is godliness, but God-likeness? And who are so like him—as those that think on his name? … Holy thoughts are the dove we send out of the ark of our souls—and they return with an olive branch of peace. Some complain that they have no joy in their lives. It is no wonder, when they are such strangers to heavenly contemplation! Would you have God give you joy and comfort—and never think of him? … Would you have your spirits cheerful? Let your thoughts be heavenly![7]

Even the insignificant details of life are opportunities for us to pause, if only for one minute. We can look into them for the Christward realities they are reflecting. Creation is God's gift to his King who has authority over all heaven and earth. And it is his gift to those co-heirs whom he has united with that King. This is not a reflection of our self-worth. It is the grace upon grace of an extravagantly kind Father for his begotten Son and his adopted sons.

Let's see into the windows of God's world and consider analogies of life *in* Christ. Let's watch how the morning sun rises over the mountains like wings hovering over the darkness and coldness of the earth. Let's remember

7 Watson, *Works of Thomas Watson*, 545–46, Kindle Edition, Location 17338. Emphasis in original.

that when Christ returns, "the sun of righteousness shall rise with healing in its wings" (Mal 4:2).

Jesus commanded us to contemplate creation and see into windows of how God cares for the material, base needs of our lives that don't seem spiritual. Let's stop to contemplate the very grass we walk on, dump waste on, and trim because of its unkempt appearance. Jesus commended it as a window to see into God's love for even those with little faith:

> Consider the lilies of the field, how they grow: they neither toil nor spin, yet I tell you, even Solomon in all his glory was not arrayed like one of these. But if God so clothes the grass of the field, which today is alive and tomorrow is thrown into the oven, will he not much more clothe you, O you of little faith? (Matt 6:28–30)

God dresses flimsy grass—here today, gone tomorrow—more impressively than the wisest man who ever lived. That same God will take care of our wardrobe. And looking into the window of common grass and flowers will remind us of that. Because Christ is our life, everything that God ordains is for our good in Christ.

Such a prayerful instinct of soul will sustain the Great Commission servant in the obscurity of thankless service. God's servant can labor in unknown fields, suffer unspoken disappointments and frustration, and practice communing with God in Christ by consciously looking into all of creation and life's experiences as windows for remembering Jesus. Such a disposition will refresh the spirituality of the gospel servant. God is with us in Christ. The nearness of God is our good. He is our great reward indeed. This assurance of his ever-present love in Christ summons us to contemplate his world and say: "Seek his presence continually" (Ps 105:4).

> *Our Lord has written the promise of resurrection, not in books alone, but in every leaf in springtime.*
>
> —Martin Luther

Chapter 5

Witness

Abiding in Christ for Loving the Lost

Scripture for Meditation

> Walk in wisdom toward outsiders, making the best use of the time. Let your speech always be gracious, seasoned with salt, so that you may know how you ought to answer each person.
>
> —Colossians 4:5–6

Some years ago, I was discussing some upcoming plans for training pastors of a Southeast Asian country. My friend, a native of that country, was the director of a facility that focused on training pastors and lay leaders. Since I was working on some translation and writing projects in his language and since many of my students came from his country, he wanted me to help out for a week.

I asked what topics had been covered in previous months and what topics they were eager to study. His answer was startling. He asked if I could teach them the Bible. I pressed him to be more specific—certain books, certain doctrines, etc.? He said they would be happy for anything from the Bible because he had yet to find a missionary who wanted to teach the Bible. He said he received multiple offers from missionaries to teach topics such as personal coaching, leadership, disciple-making movements, dental hygiene, healing prayer, conflict management, micro-enterprising, racial justice, and empowering women and children. But he glanced away and sighed, "I can't find anyone who will teach the Bible."

I don't personally know the missionaries he was recalling, but I have been around long enough to see a famine of confidence in the Bible in Great Commission service. Do such missionaries mean well? Of course, without a doubt. Are they distracted and ill-equipped? It certainly seems so. Have they adopted alternatives to evangelism and witness? Most likely.

I've heard it said that the old guard sought to convert souls by preaching the gospel, but now it's more popular to try to help people experience God's love. The Bible becomes just another resource. And the gospel then becomes an asterisk. Where the Bible is not deemed sufficient, the gospel is not esteemed as efficient. This chapter is not a criticism of gospel-adorning good works. Yet, since a disproportionate emphasis on good works can lead to mission creep and message creep, we must prioritize the supremacy of gospel proclamation. Good works and gospel preaching are good friends and not rivals. But they are also not co-equals.

Great Commission Spirituality and Blessing in Christ

Spanning the ages of Christian spirituality are two dominant categories of servants: One category comprises those who pursue God based upon the assumption that if they do well enough, understand enough, or seek earnestly enough, then they will obtain access to God. Or they will at least lay hold of his promises in incredible ways. Often their notable focus tends to be on the here and now—temporal, earthly life. They tend to fall under the categories of cultural mandate activists and great commandment agents. Another category of Great Commission servants that doesn't always attract as much attention are Great Commission ambassadors—those who focus on the announcement of the gospel and its indicatives of blessing in Christ alone, through faith alone, by grace alone.[1]

Great Commission Ambassadors

Great Commission ambassadors uniquely emphasize good works for the good of others while being unapologetically word-centered. They could be traditional missionaries, church-planters, pastors, disciple-makers, evangelists, teachers, or faithful witnesses in the secular workplace.

1 I examine these categories in chapter 5 of Burns, *Karmic Christianity*, 53–65.

Cultural mandate activists focus on action and advocacy to empower the oppressed while Great Commission ambassadors make appeals and announcements to call sinners to be reconciled to God. Great commandment agents focus on building the kingdom through good works and living like Christ while Great Commission ambassadors focus on testifying to the kingdom through good words and teaching others to look to Christ.

The gospel is not an assistance program—God helping us get better if we work hard enough in cooperation with his grace. The gospel is an announcement—God making his appeal through us that sinners can be reconciled to him through faith alone in Christ alone by grace alone. The gospel is news, not advice. The gospel is soul surgery, not a fitness program. The gospel comes to us mainly through words, grammar, syntax, and propositions. It doesn't come through works, images, symbols, and relationships. Those are indeed important. They beautifully adorn the gospel. And God can use such loving works to draw attention to gospel proclamation. But good works do not clearly or decisively communicate the gospel. During Christ's ministry, many revered him for the inclusivity of his merciful works. They also reviled him for the exclusivity of his magisterial words.

Many of us who have served in the Great Commission have been positively influenced by cultural mandate activists and great commandment agents. I certainly have. Without hesitation, I admire their acts of kindness. Yet, for some of us, living life in the "tyranny of the temporal" can wear us down. What do I mean? There is a temporality to the ministries that focus on improving the experiences of others in this life mainly through activism and good works. Don't misunderstand; I value ministries of mercy and compassion. For several years I actively served in ministries that focused on caring for orphans, prostitutes, homeless, addicts, handicapped, refugees, lepers, and marginalized social pariahs. I even helped launch a few mercy ministries.

There are incalculable opportunities for global Christians to show kindness and compassion to the strugglers and sufferers in our midst. And to be sure, the Bible commands Christians to do so. Nevertheless, the effects are fundamentally earthly (I don't mean "worldly" in an ungodly sense). To be clear, showing Christian compassion in temporal ways doesn't mean that good works are unbiblical or disobedient. And it doesn't mean that our good deeds don't matter for eternity. In a mysterious way, our holiness and good deeds in Christ truly follow us into eternity (cf. 1 Pet 2:12; Rev 14:13). Yet, they are merely transient in the earthly order. If they produce change, it doesn't last apart from souls being made new in Christ. As Jesus said, "For you always have the poor with you" (Matt 26:11). His comment acknowledges that poverty and the social effects of the curse will persist throughout every age. There will always be opportunities to help alleviate the consequences of the curse. It never goes away in this life.

But fundamental transformation only comes through being born again by the gospel of Jesus Christ. The effects and implications of the new birth affect everything in this life, though nothing in this life receives true renewal and restoration. The promised blessings are eternal, not temporal. Some future blessings spill over temporarily into the present as hints and foreshadows of what is yet to come, but they neither remain nor satisfy. That's why we groan inwardly as we wait eagerly for the return of Christ and the redemption of our bodies in the resurrection.

Such temporal blessings are not equal to eternal blessings that come only through receiving and trusting in the good news of salvation in Christ alone. Our administration of the kingdom in this life is not building it. The kingdom is not something we can touch or see; it's within us in Christ (Luke 17:20–21). We administer it by proclaiming it in the gospel of Christ.

When souls are receiving and resting in the promises of the gospel of Christ, there is the kingdom in their midst. But like our father Abraham, we must wait for God to build it:

> By faith he went to live in the land of promise, as in a foreign land, living in tents with Isaac and Jacob, heirs with him of the same promise. For he was looking forward to the city that has foundations, whose designer and builder is God. (Heb 11:9–10)

Instead of building the city of God in this life, we sojourn as nomads. No one builds the kingdom in this life; we receive the kingdom through faith alone in the King alone at his return.

The point is this: Great Commission ambassadors distinguish between good news and good works. There must be a prioritization of good words over good works. Christians should care about all suffering, and especially eternal suffering. No one escapes the wrath of God by observing good works alone. Christians should have a zeal for good works, to be sure. But they should be rightly ordered underneath good words. We must open our mouths and testify to the good news that fuels our good works. Good works indeed adorn the good news, but in gospel service, our works neither replace nor have the power of God's words. Faith comes through hearing, and hearing by the word of Christ. We are born again through the living word of God.

Spirituality and the Evangel

Biblically, evangelism is not only a spiritual gift but an office. Yet, it is a duty and privilege for all Christians. All Christians are supposed to show mercy and be hospitable, not just those who possess such gifts. Who would want to be around Christians where no one showed mercy or hospitality except for the few with those gifts? If we are evangelicals, it is only reasonable to expect that we all carry a burden for announcing the *evangel*. But we exercise that responsibility according to the unique measure of faith that God has granted each of us. None of us are the same. But we all trust in the same good news.

Some might even feel surprised that I consider witness or evangelism to be a feature of spirituality, not just service. Historically, one of the key marks of evangelical spirituality has been a devotion to the *evangel*. The historian, David Bebbington, is famous for observing the four dominant attributes of classic evangelicalism and its evangelical spirituality: biblicism, crucicentrism, conversionism, and activism—stated simply, the centrality of the Bible, the cross, conversion, and gospel outreach.

I will not outline in depth the mechanics, techniques, or tactical approaches to witnessing in the Great Commission. I have done so in previous works.[2] I have particularly designed this chapter to meditate on the abiding security of our union with Christ as we bear witness to his gospel. Living a life of witness in Christ is the result of our will being affected by the heart and convinced in the mind. When we reconsider every day that knowing Christ is infinitely good, true, and beautiful, the love of Christ will constrain us. W. C. Burns aptly mused on the love of Christ controlling our witness at all times and in all places:

---

2 Burns, *Transcultural Gospel*; Burns, *Missionary-Theologian*; Burns, "Case for the Missionary."

> Choose Him alone. This is what Enoch did, what David did, for he desired none in heaven but Him, what Peter did, for he said, Lord, to whom shall we go? What every saint is joyfully constrained by his love to do. … If you are His, you will choose Christ tonight, Christ tomorrow, Christ forever; Christ in the closet, and in the family; Christ in the shop, and in the market; Christ in the church, and in the world; Christ when you are with the godly; Christ when with the ungodly and profane; Christ in the hour of adversity; Christ, when the world smiles, and says, as it sometimes seems to do, that Christ is good; and Christ when the world frowns, and says that Christians are mad, and that Christ hath a devil. … Christ in life, Christ in death, Christ in the day of judgment, and then—ineffably glorious hope—Christ to all eternity.[3]

We will share the burning in Paul's soul: "For necessity is laid up on me. Woe to me if I do not preach the gospel!" (1 Cor 9:16). This is how a focus on witness and union with Christ affects our Great Commission service. If we are not practicing good news spirituality, then by default we are practicing good works spirituality. The former is of Christ. The latter is, in essence, of every other belief system. So evangelical spirituality essentially promotes and practices the virtue of honoring God and loving others through graciously announcing the gospel.

It seems that today's fading commitment to witness is not for lack of resources and methods, but for weak assurance in the sufficiency of Christ's word and the empowerment of his abiding presence. Abiding with Christ as we bear witness to him through his life in us is a consistent opportunity for faith, joy, and boldness in him. Ask any Great Commission servant who is active in evangelism and witness. They will likely brighten their face and recall the heavenly pleasures that wash over them when they go, stand, and speak in Christ's name. They will speak of evangelism as an occasion where they receive God's grace, much like someone who reflects on the sweetness of communion with Christ in other disciplines like prayer or meditation. Evangelism is the supernatural overflow of a soul abiding in the love of Christ.

3 Burns, *Notes of Address*, 5–6.

Our Method Corresponds to Our Message

For many of us, the absence of meditation on Scripture likely influences our casual indifference to the Bible in Great Commission service. If the Bible is merely assumed to be useful, along with other resources, it will never take the place of supremacy in Great Commission spirituality or service. If the Bible is mainly helpful, then our ministries will try to be helpful. It's not even enough to claim that the Bible should be the most important resource among many effective resources. We should esteem it in a category by itself. It is *sui generis* (of its own kind) because it is breathed out by God himself. When the voice of Scripture is silent in the mind of a gospel servant, it will remain silent in their ministry.

The word of Christ is *the* good news, not good advice, not a good story, not even just news or good news in general. It is good news of a qualitatively superior category altogether. In that sense, it is *the* exclusive good news. This good news requires a broadcast, a proclamation, an announcement. The method necessarily corresponds to the message. If we view the heart of the Bible as mainly helpful and useful for abundant living, then our ministries will seek to do the same. But if we view the heart of the Bible as the exclusive announcement of redemption from God himself, then our ministries will seek to communicate that news with gladness and gravity. For instance, a holiday party issues an invitation. The gospel proclaims a summons. As ambassadors of the *evangel*, our message demands that we broadcast the King's terms of peace.

Many spend enormous effort trying to change the temporal lives of people, and for good reasons of course. Who wouldn't want to help the impoverished, abused, diseased, and abandoned? Loving our neighbor, when we have the opportunity, requires us to care for those suffering. Yet as Christians, we should prioritize the categories of suffering. Though some might debate this, eternal suffering should always take general priority in our Great Commission efforts over temporal suffering. In the general pattern of chronic suffering under the curse, the good news should take priority over good works. They are not two sides to the same coin.

Many Great Commission servants attempt to primarily do good works (and intentionally avoid offensive topics such as sin, hell, judgment, and the exclusivity of Christ). I have heard this sentiment from multiple sincere well-intended brothers and sisters in various countries where I have taught seminars. To be honest, I've even entertained the notion myself. The explicit reason given is that unbelievers will join our Christian communities as they feel loved. And in that context of an inoffensive, positive, culturally attractive church environment, they will supposedly join us and learn to follow Jesus. So many of us care deeply about lost people. And this kind of accommodation-approach to witness is probably what we would naturally do in our workplace and families. Being accommodating works in other spheres of life. I say this not as criticism, but simply as an observation of what we automatically do. Most of us haven't been taught otherwise.

But this is fundamentally powerless. No acts of kindness are equal, more effective, or superior to the gospel of Christ. Throughout the Gospels, Jesus's own good works, signs, and wonders attracted most people. But he repelled many people when he boldly proclaimed the truth of their sinful bondage and of redemption in him alone. In other words, most unbelievers came for the miracles, the free food, the occasional healings, and the overall intrigue of a miracle-working prophet. Only those who were being born again by the word of Christ came to Christ for Christ's sake.

In obedience to the command to love our neighbor, what could be more loving than to tell them about Christ? Consider what one famous atheist, Penn Jillette, said about Christians who neglect evangelism and bearing witness to Christ's gospel. His terse rebuke should give us all reason to consider how much we love unbelievers. We should reflect on our casual treatment of the knowledge of how to escape the coming judgement:

> I've always said that I don't respect people who don't proselytize. I don't respect that at all. If you believe that there's a heaven and a hell, and people could be going to hell or not getting eternal life, and you think that it's not really worth telling them this because it would make it socially awkward—and atheists who think people shouldn't proselytize and who say just leave me along [*sic*] and keep your religion to yourself—how much do you have to hate somebody to *not* proselytize? How much do you have to hate somebody to believe everlasting life is possible and not tell them that? I mean, if I believed, beyond the shadow of a doubt, that a truck was coming at you, and you didn't believe that truck was bearing down on you, there is a certain point where I tackle you. And this is *more* important than that.[4]

4 Taylor, "How Much Do You." Emphasis in the original.

The Miracle-Working Power of the Word

Consider the account of the rich man and Lazarus in Luke 16:19–31. Two men, a rich man and a poor man, named Lazarus, knew each other in this life. The rich man overlooked the needs of the poor man. They both eventually died. Lazarus was on one side of Hades with Abraham in paradise. And the rich man? He was separated on the other side in torment. He pleaded for mercy and found none. He called out to Abraham on the other side of the chasm to send Lazarus back from Hades to warn the rich man's family to repent and flee the place of torment. Listen to the haunting interaction between the rich man and Abraham:

> But Abraham said, "They have Moses and the Prophets; let them hear them." And he said, "No, father Abraham, but if someone goes to them from the dead, they will repent." He said to him, "If they do not hear Moses and the Prophets, neither will they be convinced if someone should rise from the dead." (Luke 16:29–31)

What is Jesus saying in retelling this account? He is making a stark contrast between the efficacy of the word and all other means for influencing people toward the kingdom. Jesus is saying that an unbelieving heart is so dead and hostile to God that it cannot and will not repent. It wouldn't repent by itself even in the midst of miracles as wonderful as someone coming back from the dead. Notice he doesn't say, "neither will they be convinced *if Lazarus should warn them*." He specifically underscores the act of coming back from the dead. He's saying that if they do not believe his preaching the gospel from the Old Testament, they would neither believe even if they should see Jesus after his resurrection. That assertion has terrifying implications. That's how unable and unwilling the human heart is to believe. And that's how infallible and sufficient the word of Christ is to make us born again.

Jesus is saying that raising someone from the dead to warn of eternal torment wouldn't by itself (apart from the word) persuade sinners to repent. Since that is the case, everything else less amazing (which is basically everything) would never truly work apart from the word of Christ. It's an argument from the greater to the lesser.

Only the word can bring life into a dead heart. And in this context, Jesus is referring specifically to the power of the Old Testament as a tutor to point us to trust in the Messiah (Gal 3:24–25) Consider this: even if we have ministries of fabulously good deeds, from feeding the poor to raising the dead, if people will not heed the word of Christ, *from the Old Testament*, they will not believe the gospel message.

A popular quote has been attributed to Francis of Assisi: "Go into all the world and preach the gospel, and if necessary, use words." The sentiment here is sadly wrong. It makes as much sense as saying, "Go into all the world and feed the hungry, and if necessary, use food." The gospel is good news, words on a page, structured with propositions, grammar, and syntax. The gospel is not a life to live. Only one man lived the gospel. He alone finished it on a bloody Roman cross in Israel two thousand years ago. We live in light of his work, to be sure. But our job is to give witness to the person and work of Christ.

In Great Commission spirituality, this is our great honor and part of our inheritance in Christ. Witness is a privilege more than a task. To be an ambassador of the King to the world and to stand against the devil and his demons is a tremendous honor. We get to be on the frontlines of the expansion of the kingdom. We get to watch the gospel chase the demons out of dark lands. We get to watch Christ's word issue decrees of amnesty for all who would repent and trust in the Savior-King.

Prayerful abiding in the word of Christ, filling our souls with his words, and being always prepared to give an account of the truth is our highest duty in Great Commission spirituality. Such a prayerful inclination of abiding in Christ teaches us to rest in the power of his word. Knowing his abiding presence gives us the courage to bear witness day after day, even when the seeds seem to bounce off hard ground.

The Seed, Not the Sower

We can get up every morning, remember Jesus and his victory afresh, and go into the day that God has ordained. Wherever we go, with whomever we communicate—from our own family to our affluent neighbors, from the Muslim taxi driver to the Buddhist lady at the noodle stand—our job is to drop seeds, not mainly to attend to everyone's felt needs. They all may feel weighed down by challenges. Yet, whatever struggles they have in this life are nothing compared to what comes next. We don't know if they are thorny soil, rocky soil, or fertile soil (Matt 13:1–9). If we are discerning and wise, we may be able to develop a friendship through which we can help pull up some thorns, but no amount of friendship, evangelism, random acts of kindness, or prayer warfare can ever replace the power of the gospel of Jesus Christ.

The Bible grounds the success of the gospel in the seed of the gospel: "You have been born again, not of perishable seed but of imperishable, through the living and abiding word of God; … And this word is the good news that was preached to you" (1 Pet 1:23, 25). Even in a spiritual desert, we can trust that God's seed is sufficient. Some seeds grow quickly, others grow slowly over a lifetime. It might take a painfully long time for the seed to germinate. But seeds eventually grow after seasons of dormancy. Of course, some seeds don't bear fruit because of the ground upon which they land. That is clear from the parable of the soils (cf. Matt 13:1–9; Mark 4:3–9; Luke 8:4–8). But even though the ground looks unpromising, God can cultivate it and break it up to produce growth. Our job is to cast the seed indiscriminately and let God deal with the soil.

Consider the Mojave Desert in the Southwestern United States. It is usually oppressively hot, brown, drab, and barren. But on occasion, God sends torrential downpours that churn up the ground with deluge after deluge. Not long after the dirt settles and the sun dries up the water, small plants emerge. Dormant seeds tucked beneath the dead surface poke through. And after a short time, the desert is flush with flowers of all colors—red, yellow, blue, purple, pink, and white. Someone could go stomp seed into the desert ground. But that would not make the seed grow faster. Of course, the seed must be in the ground for flowers to blossom, but a combination of time, rain, and sun give life to the seeds.

So it is with the gospel. The power is in the seed, not the seed thrower. That doesn't give us an excuse to neglect or abuse the soils. Hardly—perhaps while we sow seed, we can remove some big rocks. But all of our hope is in our merciful Father in heaven. He alone gives growth to the seed. And as we cast the seed of the word, the power is from Christ in us to have the endurance to wait for it to bear fruit. Remembering our union with Christ helps us rest assured that it is not up to our strength to produce life and fruit. Christ is the ground, the trellis, the root, the shoot, the trunk, the head, the arms, the sap, the fruit, the sun, the rain, and the wine. Consider how the New Testament commends relying upon the power of Christ's life in us and through us for Great Commission service:

- "For I will not venture to speak of anything except what Christ has accomplished through me to bring the Gentiles to obedience—by word and deed" (Rom 15:18).
- "But by the grace of God I am what I am, and his grace toward me was not in vain. On the contrary, I worked harder than any of them, though it was not I, but the grace of God that is with me" (1 Cor 15:10).
- "Him we proclaim, warning everyone and teaching everyone with all wisdom, that we may present everyone mature in Christ. For this I toil, struggling with all his energy that he powerfully works within me" (Col 1:28–29).
- "Whoever serves, as one who serves by the strength that God supplies—in order that in everything God may be glorified through Jesus Christ" (1 Pet 4:11).

Love without Truth

The Bible gives three possible reactions to a clear and accurate announcement of the gospel: it is either foolishness, offensive, or good news. Take note if an unbeliever doesn't respond in one of these three ways, but instead responds, "thanks for the advice" or "it's nice to hear what Christians believe," or "I'm glad that all worked for you." Did we communicate the gospel as insight for living a better life? Simply an explanation of Christian doctrine? Or our own personal path to finding happiness? If that is how we explain it, we have not rightly communicated the good news as *the* truth. The gospel is *the* truth for salvation, not *a* truth among many others. It is true whether only one person or the whole world believes it.

Often the error in our witness comes from what we do not say more than what we actually say. With a good desire to show love and speak truth, some of us might make qualifications for every statement in order to be deferential, polite, or sensitive: "Well, that's just my experience." Or, "that's just what Christians believe."

We shouldn't merely *share* the gospel as though it were an amicable topic of discussion. We must *declare* the gospel because it is a hopeful message of amnesty from the returning King. Sometimes in our casual gospel conversations, we need to lean across the coffee table and look our friend in the eye with humility and honesty. We need to speak clearly like Nathan did to David. After telling David the story of the rich man who took the poor man's lamb, Nathan asserted bluntly: "You are the man!" (2 Sam 12:7). Gospel proclamation should lay claim on its hearers. We might presume that our timidity (which we think of as humility) communicates grace and love. But obscuring the truth is neither grace nor love. Love without truth is disingenuous and therefore unloving.

Truth without Love

On the other hand, focusing exclusively on the truth and persuasion can muddle the gospel. We must beware lest the good news no longer sounds gracious. The kindness of the message can be clouded by the coarseness of the messenger. This happens when we lob the gospel like a grenade rather than a seed. Grenades make an impact immediately and forcefully. Seeds grow imperceptibly and sprout apart from the effort of the sower. One brings death, the other brings life.

Those of us who are staunch defenders of truth, even if we manage not to come across as self-righteous, can still tend to overstate one part of the truth in a way that eclipses the grace of Christ. Again, our error here is in what elements of the truth we leave out in favor of others.

This can look like emphasizing sin and lostness, leaving our hearers with an impression that the gospel call is exclusively repentance. Highlighting man's imperfection in light of God's word is essential. But a call only to repentance is insufficient. It leaves the questions, "How much repentance? How sorry do I need to be for my sin? When do I know I have surrendered all? How can I be sure?" The answer lies in the fact that our surety is in the satisfaction of God in Christ's work on our behalf. Our surety is not in our surrender, our sincerity, or the degrees of remorse over our sin. Our assurance is in the objective, external work of Christ for us on a Roman cross, in an empty tomb two thousand years ago. Repentance is the fruit of trusting in Christ alone.

Love with Truth, Truth in Love

Isn't it amazing that the kindness of God is meant to lead us to repentance (Rom 2:4)? That doesn't mean God's kindness foregoes conviction. People repent upon seeing "the riches of his kindness and forbearance and patience" (Rom 2:4) because they realize they have no hope to "escape the judgment of God" (Rom 2:3) apart from the mercy of God.

Telling the truth in love does not mean communicating God's blind approval or tolerance of sexual decadence, lying, cheating, love of money, idolatrous self-expression, or the pursuit of self-discovery. Loving people with the truth demands that we tell them the specifics of what it means to be loved by God. Then, and only then, can the kindness of God truly lead them to repentance.

No oncologist who should prescribe immediate brain surgery for an aggressive tumor would give qualifications like, "that's just what I believe," or "you can just get a scalp massage if that works for you." The doctor isn't offering a helpful suggestion. Any news to the cancer patient that is intentionally ambiguous, unpersuasive, and casual is patently unkind. It is medical malpractice. Telling the truth is loving. Loving is telling the truth. Giving grace is giving good news.

The Bible explains the love of God: "But God shows his love for us in that while were still sinners, Christ died for us" (Rom 5:8); and "In this is love, not that we have loved God but that he loved us and sent his Son to be the propitiation for our sins" (1 John 4:10). God loves to forgive Adam's rebellious progeny. God loves to honor shameful pariahs. God loves to set free souls in bondage to sin. God loves to raise up souls dead in sin. God loves to bestow peace upon souls overcome by fear. In love God united us to Christ in his death and resurrection. He was pleased to crush and then raise up the Son for us.

Precept and Promise

The law-grace approach of the Protestant Reformation is quite simple and basic for telling the truth in love. This approach wounds the conscience with the law. It heals the soul with the gospel. Sinners can have their consciences so seared that they call evil good and good evil. They need to look into the mirror of God's standards to see how they don't measure up. It can take a long time for their eyes to be opened and for them to see the truth as good news. Slowly the law and the gospel are at work, even when they don't know it.

Others still have sensitive consciences, and the light of nature and the law on their souls already condemn them. They might receive the gospel quickly because their conscience has already been condemning them. What God commands in his precepts, he graciously bestows in his promises. God's standards show us our sin and send us to our Savior. Then united with Christ, God's precepts tell us how to walk honorably in gratitude to God. As Augustine notably prayed, "Give me the grace to do as you command, and command me to do what you will!"[5]

The human conscience knows its sin. Even the most hardened atheist in their dying hours of hospice care senses that they are in terrible trouble. Somebody somewhere beyond the grave has been surveilling their secrets. The atheist knows they are about to pay for it. But it is the Spirit's job to do that convicting work, not ours. We must give sinners the free offer of grace in Christ. No preconditions necessary.

Curious Evangelism and Image-Bearers

Evangelism and discipleship should share the same Christ-centered principles but with differing tactics. In both, our job is to influence people to Christ. We do this in the kind way of Christ, with the convicting and comforting word of Christ while emphasizing the complete work of Christ. Paul says, "Walk in wisdom toward outsiders, making the best use of the time. Let your speech always be gracious, seasoned with salt, so that you may know how you ought to answer each person" (Col 4:5–6).

In witnessing, we need to be discerning, kind, and intentional. We probably won't see a conversion every time, or even most times. That is up to the Holy Spirit, not us. We must be content to keep planting seeds. Jesus will bring in the harvest. Maybe all we can offer someone is a helpful Christ-proclaiming conversation that the Holy Spirit reminds them of later in life. Maybe they'll remember it when they get their terminal diagnosis, or when their life is slipping away underneath the crushing impact of a car wreck. We never know how quickly the dormant seeds of the gospel can shoot up when the Spirit gives them sufficient rain and sun.

The Lord is sensitive to our felt needs and kindly brings us to our deeper spiritual needs. We should try to discern how God might be chipping away at an unbeliever's fortifications against the knowledge of him. Showing genuine interest and thoughtful curiosity is a powerful way to get people

5 Augustine, *Confessions*, 233.

talking. I call this "curious evangelism." People and the purposes of God are interesting if we look into their lives enough. This is how contemplation serves our witness. A sanctified curiosity can serve virtue. It can get us outside of ourselves and help us look into people's lives with Christian compassion and attentiveness. G. K. Chesterton commented once that there are no uninteresting things, only uninterested people.

Let's take the time to contemplate the people God puts in our lives, blemishes and all. Then we might begin to see their tragic stories as fallen image bearers to be peculiarly fascinating. Listen to how they retell their life drama. Listen for the characters—the protagonists and antagonists, those whom they love and those whom they hate. And remember that every person's life story will have one of two final resolutions: (1) all their best dreams will come true in Christ, and they will live happily ever after with him in the truest of true fairytales; or (2) all their worst nightmares will come true, and they will suffer torment forever with the devil in the worst tragedies.

Let unbelievers open doors one comment and question at a time. Walk through them and see how far you can get into the rooms of their lives and memories. Always be ready to introduce them to Jesus. The cross of Christ is the comedy par excellence that turns the conflict of sin on its head. It mocks the antagonistic dragon, and it recasts the most unlikely rebels into righteous royalty to whom God gladly bestows his kingdom.

Jesus, the Great Soul Physician

Consider how Jesus, in three consecutive chapters in John, sensitively approached different individuals. He listened to each individual's life, their questions, their needs, and replied with a theological answer that corresponded to how they opened the door of conversation.

In John 3, Jesus meets Nicodemus under the cover of night. Nicodemus is a religious leader with a burning theological question. Jesus answers in kind with a metaphor of birth—the need to be born again. And he goes on to further answer Nicodemus's theological inquiries.

In the next chapter, Jesus meets the Samaritan woman at the well. The well was a common place in the Old Testament where unmarried people would meet. As a rabbi he is breaking both social and cultural conventions to reach out to a Samaritan woman. Since she's drawing water, Jesus uses water as a theological metaphor. He points to how the Messiah will slake the thirst of anyone who drinks from the water of eternal life. During their conversation, the woman's checkered past with men comes up. Jesus acknowledges her shame. But he points beyond it to reveal himself as her Messiah.

In the fifth chapter of John, Jesus stumbles upon a sick man at the Pool of Bethesda, which ironically translates to "house of mercy." He takes note of the man's thirty-eight-years-long battle with infirmities. The man was trapped in the superstitious traditions foisted upon the invalids. Crippled people languished at the pool for someone to stir up the healing waters and dip them in. This man's miracle cure was deferred most of his life. No one cared, not just once or twice, but year after year. But on that day, Jesus cared. He used the man's weakness, the abuse of a religious system, and the coldness of others to point him to the kingdom.

In each of these accounts, Jesus's diagnosis is perceptive. He is decisive and exacting. Like a good soul physician, he steps around social, religious, and cultural conventions to speak to the heart of each individual. His kindness and love were the language that transcended those conventions. He addressed each person in their humanity. He expressed compassion for their felt earthly needs, but never let it stay there. He tactfully and deftly moved beyond their felt needs to their true eternal needs for a Savior.

Based upon their backgrounds, each individual's thirst for salvation looked different. They had all misdiagnosed their own issues. But Jesus saw through those barriers to the deeper, eternal issues at stake. Chronically ill patients might self-diagnose themselves based on their unique combination of complex symptoms. But a good physician cuts through the fog of symptoms and identifies the underlying problem.

Uniquely Drawn to Christ

Jesus is the exclusive way to salvation, indeed. But for all of us, the road that leads us to Jesus relates to our individual history and humanity. Jesus is the exclusive way to the Father, but initially we each find ourselves on different paths to Jesus. This doesn't mean there are other ways to salvation outside of Christ and his gospel—I am not promoting Christian inclusivism. The point is that the spirit of God is working with sinners individually in their unique contexts. He is wooing and drawing sinners to Christ differently. From doubters and divorcees, to the disabled or depressed, to drunkards and the dying, Christ calls us to himself individually.

Some, like Nicodemus, are pulled to Christ intellectually; they desire theological answers. They long for what is true. Others, like the Samaritan woman are wooed to Christ emotionally. They desire to love and be loved. They long to rejoice in what is beautiful. While those like the man at the pool, afflicted and rejected, are drawn to Christ by the felt need for restoration. They groan inwardly because the good of creation suffers under the shattering weight of the curse. They long for the renewal of what was originally good. Everything inside them cries, "It wasn't supposed to be this way!"

The Holy Spirit might draw each of us to Christ differently in those initial stages of effectual calling. He might use tragedies, various points of conviction, or a broken heart. He might accentuate the dissatisfying claims of naturalistic and materialistic worldviews, wearisome besetting sins, and layers of shame, fear, bondage, weakness, and guilt. These are the initial headwaters that flow to Jesus. But Jesus is the only river that carries us to the ocean of the Father's love. We all have the same original problem in Adam. Jesus is the exclusive solution.

The Way, the Truth, and the Life

In witnessing, we should remember every major religious and belief system in the world basically has three common features. Christian philosophers, theologians, and missiologists have recognized that every belief system has a notion of transcendence, a moral code that can attain some kind of paradise or *telos*, and some sort of divine entity that communicates and enforces that moral code. Every belief system is the product of like-minded people who have systematized what is deeply imbedded in all our hearts.

But Christianity is different from all others. It claims that the Creator commanded a moral standard, yet fulfilled it and its penalties himself. He did so to make a way to paradise with him for all who would simply receive his gift.

As our Priest, Jesus made the way to a life of paradise in him as our King, through receiving and resting in his truth as our Prophet. There is none righteous, so moralism fails. But Jesus is our Priest who fulfills the law's requirements and penalties for us. There is no one who understands, so speculation fails. But Jesus is our Prophet who proclaims the mysteries of the gospel. And there is no one who seeks God, so, mysticism fails. But Jesus is our King who secures our life in God.

Home, Belonging, and Wholeness

Though there is collegial debate on this point, I have made the case in previous works that there are four common belief systems in most cultures that emerge from a guilt/righteousness paradigm fundamentally imbedded in our humanity: shame/honor, fear/peace, bondage/freedom, and weakness/strength.[6]

Most cultures borrow predominantly from one of these beliefs systems, while borrowing from all four to some degree. Everyone wants honor. No one wants to be shameful. Everyone wants peace. No one wants to live in fear. Everyone wants to be free. No one wants to languish in bondage. Everyone wants to be strong. No one wants to suffer weakness or poverty. These are all consequential problems from our deepest problem in Adam: guilt. And the only way to solve that problem is through receiving the last Adam's righteousness through faith alone. Upon being declared righteous in union with Christ, God bestows on us honor. God establishes peace with us. God sets us free from sin and the devil. And God makes us strong and abounding in Christ.

Furthermore, most belief systems explicitly and all humans implicitly share similar longings of the soul. We all long for the good, the true, and the beautiful. We can observe these in three analogies—the longing to be home (the good), the longing to be whole (the true), and the longing to belong (the beautiful). There are likely more than these three (e.g., longing for honor, peace, freedom, and strength), but Christian theologians, philosophers, apologists, and historians throughout the centuries have generally acknowledged these three, or analogies like them.[7] For the purposes of this chapter, these three longings will be in view.

6 See Burns, *Transcultural Gospel*; Burns, *Ancient Gospel*. In these works, I demonstrate that the guilt/righteousness paradigm is rooted in the Hebrew Bible (and also in the Mishna, which details the Jewish expectation of the imputation of merits), whereas the well-known guilt/innocence paradigm emerges popularly from post-Enlightenment social theory in the West.

7 For similar observations but different formulations of these longings, see Root and Guthrie, *Sacrament of Evangelism*. I am grateful for the privilege of being discipled in evangelism and apologetics by Jerry Root. Some of my observations in this section grow out of his wise influence and intentional mentorship during those early years of campus evangelism. He showed me how to see people with curiosity and compassion.

When these desires awaken within us, we inevitably attach value to the object of those desires. Yet they leave us severely disillusioned. God gives us good things in this life, but they are never ultimately satisfying. They are merely humble custodians opening the windows of the soul. They help us glimpse the elusive joy of heaven. When we give our hearts' devotion to that which is good but not God, our idolatry betrays us and breaks our hearts anew. But God can use that angst to drive us to himself. Here biblical contemplation in Christ serves our Great Commission spirituality and witness. It helps us see people in the nitty-gritty of their lostness. We can sympathize as helpful conversationalists, influencing them to see the kindness of God.

Home

First, there is the longing to be home. Home represents all that is good, all that is well—happiness, flourishing, security, and prosperity. It's imbedded in our classic stories. Consider Ulysses in *The Odyssey* who wished to go home to Ithaca to be with his wife. We see it in Virgil's *Aeneid* where Aeneas aches for Troy that has fallen and looks forward to building Rome. Or consider Tolkien's hobbits off on adventures, only to return to the Shire—there and back again. Modern stories share the same longing for home. Consider Maximus in the movie, *Gladiator*, fighting to return to the farm with his wife and son. Think of William Wallace of *Braveheart*, warring for freedom so that his home in Scotland may flourish once again in peace.

Everyone knows there is something transcendent in the feeling of being home. When we are away from home, we reminisce about the smells, the sounds, the flavors, the laughter, the warmth, and the overall sense of stability. All is well. All shall be well when we are home. But upon returning to wherever we call home in our child-like memories, what happens inside of us? Disappointments abound. The old house is dilapidated. Mom and dad, if they are still alive, are wearing the years heavy on their faces. Ornate buildings are razed and replaced with modern ones. The meadows and woodlands have been conquered by sprawling shopping centers. And worst of all, no one we used to know is around anymore. Yes, we are "home." But our heart is not. Chesterton well observed that we are all truly pilgrims at home. Something tells us that we were made for a better world. A better home. A better country. With a better King.

Belong

Second, there is the longing to belong. Similar to a longing to be safe and secure in the familiarity of home, there is that desire to know and be known, truly and deeply. This is a romantic longing—though not necessarily in the erotic sense. It's a desire to be swallowed up in the beautiful, to desire someone and to be reciprocally desired by them.

We see this desire expressed in literature and movies, like *Forrest Gump*. Jenny, the object of Forrest Gump's lifelong affection, refuses to let him love her. She chases after abusive, phony lovers instead. Fearing that the intimate belonging she craves can only be found in a handicapped man, and ashamed at the ugliness of her life and soul, she runs from him. The irony is that *running* is precisely what his love for her compels him to do throughout the movie. Fear and shame keep her from receiving his acceptance. But in the end, his marathon-like love wins her heart.

Every time we latch onto a new relationship—a friend, a lover, or a family member—we hope they will love us. And we give ourselves in love to them. But the closer we get, the more clearly we see their soul warts. And they see ours. The garbage of our souls stinks up the relationship. The disillusionment, irritation, and pushback give way to a slow death. The youthful romance fizzles. And the scar tissue on the heart grows thick. It's nearly impenetrable. Even with the best of relationships, something of God's image in us wants to belong perfectly, freely, fully, and forever. Something tells us that we were made for a better family, a better brother, a better lover, a better friend, and a better father. All human loves are but faint echoes of God's true, archetypical love.

This longing is what God historically used to woo Augustine to Christ. Augustine said he was in love with the beauty of love but never found love. In *Confessions* III.1, he says, "I had not yet fallen in love, but I was in love with the idea of it. ... I began to look around for some object for my love, since I badly wanted to love something."[8] Later, in *Confessions* X.27, he saw that the love of God was the evasive beauty of love that he had been chasing in the "hissing cauldron of lust"[9] in Carthage:

---

8 Augustine, *Confessions*, 55. An alternative translation of the Latin is: "I was not yet in love, yet I loved to love. ... I sought what I might love, in love with loving."

9 Augustine, 55.

> I have learnt to love you late, Beauty at once so ancient and so new! I have learnt to love you late! You were within me, and I was in the world outside myself. I searched for you outside myself and, disfigured as I was, I fell upon the lovely things of your creation. You were with me, but I was not with you. The beautiful things of this world kept me far from you and yet, if they had not been in you, they would have had no being at all. You called me; you cried aloud to me; you broke my barrier of deafness. You shone upon me; your radiance enveloped me; you put my blindness to flight. You shed your fragrance about me; I drew breath and now I gasp for your sweet odour. Tasted you, and now I hunger and thirst for you. You touched me, and I am inflamed with love of your peace.[10]

Whole

Third, there is the longing to be whole. One language that transcends every culture is the language of love and forgiveness. Organically related to the longings for home and belonging is the longing to have the pieces of our sinful lives put back together. Any of us who have lived an honest year of life knows that we want to be loved. And we want to love someone. But the problem is, we know we need forgiveness. Every new habit, therapist, job, diet, and resolution we try fails to deliver on its promises. We know that if we are truly known, we would be revealed to be unlovely and unlovable. We are afraid of what people might see if we let anyone get close enough to us. We might be afraid of what they would *not* see in us. We might be afraid of letting ourselves get so close to true love only to suddenly lose it forever.

In the movie, *Good Will Hunting*, Will Hunting masks memories of childhood abuse and abandonment with a smart, tough-guy façade. As his counselor perceptively probes into the dark basement rooms of his life, Will stumbles into nightmares he never wanted to revisit. He lets himself remember the shame of those events. There, in the safety of that relationship, he could deal with the sin that was perpetrated upon him and now controls him.

We all, to some degree, operate in guarded ways to anesthetize the pain of broken dreams. We react in insecurity of unsatisfied desires

10 Augustine, 231–32.

and the fear of future rejection. The broken pieces of our lives litter our memories with regrets. This longing to be whole and restored to our original innocence before Adam's sin pushes many of us onto the treadmill of self-improvement. We chase after religious rituals, pilgrimages, spiritual retreats, yogic meditation, natural remedies, and the like. We know we need someone outside of us to put our pieces back together again.

What is the problem with all these legitimate feelings of brokenness? They are not our deepest problem. Emotionally they feel ultimate. But theologically they are penultimate. They are tremors and aftershocks of the earthquake of sin that has separated us from God and hurled us out of his blessed presence.

Yet, what we perceive to be our original problem determines the solutions we pursue. As Great Commission servants, we never want to inadvertently communicate to our unbelieving friends that we agree that their perceived problems are their deepest problems. True, they are struggling and suffering. And we must express Christian compassion, not a contrived affectation. But we must also remember that their struggles in this life are because they are Adam's cursed progeny. They share in Adam's federal condemnation and corrupt nature. Our goal is to kindly and compassionately listen to their stories. And then we should seek to use their experiences as open doors to bring in the light and the love of the gospel. Unbelievers are dead in their trespasses—not merely sick, wounded, or oppressed.

A Prayerful Instinct to Bear Witness in Christ

In 1 Corinthians 15:58, Paul calls our service "the work of the Lord" (it is *his* work). He says "our labor" (we actively participate) is "in him" (in union with him). And that labor in Christ is "never in vain" (his sufficient word will accomplish his sovereign will). Let us, then, "be steadfast, immovable, always abounding in the work of the Lord."

As we prayerfully abide in Christ and compassionately contemplate the lostness of people around us, the joy and boldness that God gives is astonishing. It can feel like the warm spring winds melting the snow after a long, dark winter. That instinct of prayerfulness that consciously meditates on the word of Christ and rests in union with him supplies us with that joy and boldness. Witnessing is less intimidating when we are content in God.

When the love of Christ constrains us, techniques and tactics are important but not determinative. If God can speak through Balaam's donkey, he can speak through you and me. We can rest in God and get busy in his harvest.

Every attempt to influence others to Christ in his kindness, with his convicting and comforting word, emphasizing his complete work, is an occasion for joy in Christ. We get to identify with and speak on behalf of the King. We get to be with him as he ransoms people from every tribe, tongue, and nation. Remember the kindness of God. Rest in your union with Christ. Live like God is sovereign.

> *I believe that much of the secret of soul-winning lies in having bowels of compassion, in having spirits that can be touched with the feeling of human infirmities.*
>
> —Charles Spurgeon

Chapter 6

Humility

Abiding in Christ, Assured by His Love

Scripture for Meditation

> He humbled you and let you hunger and fed you with manna, which you did not know, nor did your fathers know, that he might make you know that man does not live by bread alone, but man lives by every word that comes from the mouth of the Lord.
>
> —Deuteronomy 8:3

During the first years of ministry, I remember being at a prayer meeting for the nations and praying aloud with sincere fervency, "Lord, humble me." A much wiser, seasoned saint kindly took me aside later and reminded me that the Bible commands us to humble ourselves (Jas 4:10). The Bible does not tell us to pray that God himself would humble us. It is a fearful thing to undergo God's humbling (2 Cor 12:21). "God opposes the proud, but gives grace to the humble" (Jas 4:6). God has indeed taught me humility me over the years, and he has been incredibly gracious as well.

To continue to see how resting in union with Christ for Great Commission spirituality and service works itself out, we must consider the roots and implications of biblical humility. We must also unpack its adversary—pride. This chapter will start to weave together threads from the previous chapters. It will show how they tie together with the remaining chapter for growing virtuously in union with Christ.

Humility and pride are contrasted throughout Scripture. It seems, however, that both are only partially understood because we tend to look at external actions, words, and behaviors as indicative of humility or pride. Therefore, we focus on saying the right words to appear humble—"Thank you for the compliment, but it was really God working through me." Or "Here's the dish I made for the church potluck, but it's really not that good. I'm not a great chef." We are also alert to behaviors of pride, in others of course—"Did you see how the conference speaker was so arrogant before his talk? He just walked up there, opened his Bible, never prayed, and never even greeted the audience." Or "I just don't understand how the pastor can talk so dogmatically and confidently about the Bible. He leaves no room for questions, conversation, or imagination." We've all heard comments like these. And we have probably said similar things as well—I know I have.

Humility and Honesty

Humility is a strange virtue. If we are meeting with someone for accountability or discipleship, maybe it's not uncommon to say, "I'm working on self-control," or "I'm grateful the Lord has helped me grow in love and gentleness." But as soon as we say, "I've been growing in humility lately," we castigate ourselves for even saying such a prideful thing! Or our accountability partners probably snicker to themselves with the same thoughts.

As soon as we refer to ourselves and humility in the same sentence, we disprove our case. Humility is one of those virtues that no one wants to talk about because it's so elusive. It's either confused with a mild, stoic temperament, or a self-loathing, melancholic one. We might be good at policing external actions, words, body language, and public decorum in order to look humble, but that can all be false humility. Now no one would readily admit that they are trying to be deceptive and putting on an act. Sometimes we are unaware of our false humility. Other times we are just not honest about it. Sadly, all these caricatures skew the heart of humility.

True humility, rightly understood as rooted in our assurance in Christ, produces otherworldly peace. It soothes every sensitive part of our spirituality and service. The virtue of humility creates a context where we can receive God's healing and help. In humility, God restores us in our security in Christ. He then reinforces our resolve to serve well for the long haul. He gives grace to the humble.

As C. S. Lewis popularly observed, humility is free to be truthful about both the good and the bad. It's about having an honest opinion rather than a lowly opinion of ourselves. He called it, "self-forgetfulness."[1] This is not because we don't care and prefer to neglect ourselves. That's just another manifestation of false humility. True humility is placing appropriate value on the truth of the matter. In other words, humility is rightly ordered honesty. The ancients often paired the virtue of humility with the virtue of honesty—two sides of the same coin. We can't have genuine humility without naked honesty. Are we scoundrels deserving of hell? Yes, to be sure. Sin spoils even our most earnest obedience and purest motives. Our best efforts would condemn us to hell apart from our union with Christ. It's all completely insufficient for earning righteousness.

While such a bleak prognosis is true, it's not the whole picture of how God made us. Jesus asked the rhetorical question, "If you then, who are evil, know how to give good gifts to your children, how much more will your Father who is in heaven give good things to those who ask him!" (Matt 7:11). In other words, even evil people possess the capacity and the goodwill to do good. And since that is the case, our righteous Father in heaven has no limits to his goodwill and capacity to show us kindness. These are two honest statements, both rightly ordered. Mankind is indeed evil and resists God's grace every day. Yet, we still have the capacity and goodwill to build sturdy bridges, serve in hospice care, throw our bodies on grenades for our comrades, pen impartial laws, nurture newborns, and chisel sublime sculptures from marble that stir the heart.

All those deeds of goodness fall short of meriting God's righteous standard. God's goodness is ontological, meaning, it comes from his being. It's who he is. His benevolence and love for us is immutable and impassible; he never changes with emotions like we do. His goodness comes from who he is, not how he feels based upon our faithfulness. His lovingkindness is constant. Full and fixed.

---

1 See Lewis, *Screwtape Letters*, 66, 69–73; Lewis, *Mere Christianity*, 125. For a great resource on these themes of humility and self-forgetfulness in Lewis's writings, see Rigney, *Lewis on the Christian*.

Biblical humility is honest about these things—a true estimation of who we are and of who God is. We are sinners in Adam, condemned and corrupt. But we can still do non-meritorious good things according to the image of God. It's not a sin to accept compliments and congratulations. It's a good thing to rejoice in our victories and accomplishments. In God's common grace all people can find pleasure in the work of their hands. Neither is it a problem to admit our need for growth and the fact that we don't always have it all right. It's okay to be a brainy intellectual, but it's equally okay to admit we have more to learn. God speaks to us with absolute truth. But who has the mind of God? Can anyone presume to know God absolutely? Finite minds have much to learn from our infinite God for all eternity.

Union with Christ Humbles Us and Helps Us

Here is how our union with Christ helps us in our humility and service. When we give ourselves to reaching the unreached or teaching the undiscipled, we are tempted to either feel good about ourselves in a self-congratulatory way, or to receive the admiration from other Christians as an echo of our worth and special approval from God. In other words, we can let our Great Commission service go to our heads. On the other hand, when we spend our lives in Christ's service, we are tempted to criticize ourselves for not doing enough or not producing enough fruit. We are also tempted to interpret people's disinterest and casualness as echoes of our worthlessness and disapproval from God.

However, when we consciously remember our union with Christ, we can honestly admit that though sin stains all we do, our imperfection does not have the final word. Through faith in Christ, our labor is never in vain. Never. God receives and will reward our steadfast, immovable, abounding labor in Christ. Not because we are so good, but because our service is *in* Christ. He is our Mediator, Intercessor, and Advocate. He is our Vine, the source of our life and the supply of our fruit. If it pleases Christ to give us light or heavy responsibilities, then we bless his name. We trust him to give us strength. And if it pleases Christ for us to bear little or much fruit, then we bless his name. We trust him to get all the glory.

Humility is honest both about who we were in Adam and the effects of sin. It is also honest about who we are in Christ and his sanctifying effects.

It speaks openly about our soul warts and wrinkles from Adam's nature. But it would be false humility to not tell the whole truth. Humility also goes on to rejoice and rest in who we are in our new nature with all the beauty and honor of Christ breaking through from union with him. There is a peacefulness to this honesty. It is the peace of Christ. It is a transcendent peacefulness that rests in him. And for high-anxiety, high-risk assignments on the frontlines, we must maintain an honest, humble assessment of who we are in Christ and who Christ is for us. This is why union with Christ is immeasurably applicable for our Great Commission spirituality.

Pride and Disbelief

Some Christian philosophers, such as Augustine, have posited that pride is the first and root cause of sin. This kind of pride is not the natural satisfaction of a worthy accomplishment or in the success of a child. This kind of pride is disordered, sinful pride. To be sure, Adam proudly disobeyed God. And he neglected to guide Eve away from the serpent's deception. But there might be something deeper and more substantive beneath surface-level pride.

Pride emerges out of some sort of pretention—that my way is better than God's way, or that my way is Yahweh. I believe my way, law, code, rule, system, or custom is better than God's. It's not that pride is lawless. Pride says: "I am a law unto myself. I am independent of God and his word." Pride is not anti-law. Pride is pro-law—either a self-made law or a legalistic distortion of God's law. In both cases, pride is anti-grace—it resists God's grace and replaces God's grace. Just as in the parable of the prodigal son (Luke 15:11–32), the rebellious son resisted his father's grace and sought freedom his own way, and the religious son replaced the father's grace and sought honor his own way.[2]

John Calvin is helpful in unpacking the root of sin. He dismisses the assumption that Adam's sin was mere intemperance or lack of self-control, and says in response, "We ought therefore look more deeply."[3] Calvin agrees in part with Augustine that pride was the first sin: "Indeed, Augustine speaks rightly when he declares that pride was the beginning of all evils. For if ambition [that is, ambitious pride or pretense] had not

2 I unpack the anti-grace hearts of both sons in this parable in Burns, *Ancient Gospel*, 361–71.

3 Calvin, *Institutes*, 419.

raised man higher than was meet and right, he could have remained in his original state."[4]

Calvin goes on to argue, however, that "a fuller definition from the nature of the temptation" demonstrates that Adam held God's word in contempt through irreverence for God and disbelief. He says, "Unfaithfulness, then, was the root of the Fall. But thereafter ambition and pride, together with ungratefulness, arose. ... Faithlessness opened the door to ambition."[5]

Calvin explains that Adam was unfaithful to God because "he had disbelieved in God's Word," and he refused to accept "that the ultimate goal of the happy life is to be loved by [God]." Spurning God's love "extinguished the whole glory of God."[6] Therefore, at the root of sin, underneath pride and pretense, is a disbelief in what God declares about his love and glory.

Unfaithfulness to God's word shows a pretentious disbelief in God's love, which ultimately brings immense dishonor upon his good name. And Calvin insightfully employed the word, "disbelief," over against the more common, "unbelief." Disbelief implies the refusal to believe and receive something wonderful. But unbelief suggests a state of not believing, possibly based upon a rejection of the truth, but possibly out of sheer ignorance or forgetfulness.

What about the pretense of independence from God? What is its origin? The Bible says that "the love of money is a root of all kinds of evils" (1 Tim 6:10). Indeed, money is not bad, just the love and devotion to money. This doesn't mean that gold or fiat currency creates sin. The problem is when a soul heartily trusts in and loves the *power* of purchasing whatever money can buy. Such a devotion to purchasing power produces all kinds of evils.

We love money when we put our confidence in our financial security. We rest in our independence from God, able to purchase all that we want. We find ourselves serving our autonomy from God. Money is just the tool for autonomy. We love how money makes us feel secure, provided for, and free to do what we want. We love what we trust in, and we serve what we love. Jesus said it best: "No one can serve two masters, for either he will hate the one and love the other, or he will be devoted to the one and despise the other. You cannot serve God and money" (Matt 6:24).

---

4 Calvin, 419–20.

5 Calvin, 420.

6 Calvin, 421.

Our trust in, love for, and service to anything (of which money is a mere symbol) that is not God is fundamentally rooted in pretentious disbelief of God's word—disbelieving who God is, what he requires, and what he promises. This is not merely for lack of information about God. In Adam's corruption, disbelief is the prevailing disposition of our hearts apart from Christ. We disbelieve what we know of God in creation and what we understand of God in Scripture. It's our fallen nature apart from Christ.

We obey what we love, and we love what we believe. According to the Protestant Reformation's formulation of *sola fide*, faith, or belief, requires knowledge (*notitia*), assent (*assensus*), and a hearty trust (*fiducia*). This is an analogy for how belief simply works: Suppose I was severely dehydrated and found a bottle of purified water. I know that it is water. I assent that it pure and essential for my life. I trust and receive it by drinking it without adding anything to it to improve or ensure its purity. My belief in the water is not complete by my knowledge and assent. I must heartily drink it down as though my life depends upon it. It is possible to know and assent to the truths of the gospel but not trust in them. Even the demons know and acknowledge the truth but don't receive it or trust in it (Jas 2:19).

Imperfect Love Creates Fear

What keeps the unregenerate soul back from receiving Christ and resting in him for salvation? On the surface it might look like pride and pretention. But it's more than that. The bad news of the law must first break us before the good news of grace can heal us. Once we are convicted by God's unmet standards and see our need, what is the main issue that keeps us from faith and repentance? When people repent for fear of judgment, their obligatory "sorry" is based on a "worldly grief" (2 Cor 7:10). But this is merely a fearful, legal repentance. Yet, the goodness of the gospel creates a peaceful, evangelical repentance based on "godly grief" (2 Cor 7:10).

The Bible teaches that the *kindness* of God is meant to lead unbelievers to repentance (Rom 2:4). Why kindness and benevolence, not just sheer command and omnipotence? It suggests that something holds us back from repenting. Only the kindness and love of God can conquer it. All sinners put up a wall that only God's lovingkindness can break down.

What holds us back from repentance after conviction that only God's kindness can overcome? John's first epistle says, "There is no fear in love, but perfect love casts out fear. For fear has to do with punishment, and whoever fears has not been perfected in love" (1 John 4:18). In Adam, our problem of disbelief and pride is rooted in fear. Disordered fear. Counterfeit fear. Maybe fear of admitting we are bad and shameful. Maybe fear of what might happen to our job or family if we change our religion. Maybe unwarranted fear of false ideas of God himself.

The Bible teaches that a rightly ordered fear of God in the context of his love in Christ is a worshipful privilege for the saint. It is the path to wisdom. But the enemy has ways of twisting God's word. The devil can deceive us into feeling fear from disbelief in God's goodness and love. That is how the he tempted our first parents in the garden. Yet, when the lovingkindness of God comes flooding in, it extinguishes our fear. More than that, it exhausts our fear. The grace of God overcomes and absorbs it.

So, the battle for Great Commission spirituality for the sake of Great Commission service comes back to the most basic of all Sunday school lessons: "God is love." Since God's perfect love casts out fear, then its alternative must be true also: imperfect love creates fear. This could include false assumptions and incomplete theology about God's love. Or it could be that we project upon God the imperfect love we have received (and maybe even suffered) at the hands of those who should have loved us the most. It could have been that easily enraged father, that petty, malcontent mother, that abusive uncle, that adulterous fiancé, or that rebellious child. It's not that God's love is imperfect; it's just that our understanding or our interpretation of his love is imperfect.

To anesthetize the fear of pain and rejection, we put up pretenses. We operate in ways that are devoid of true humility and honesty. If we are remotely aware of our face-saving tendencies, we might recognize the patterns of pretense in our lives. So, we work on "not being prideful." This can look like qualifying our statements with Christian jargon, putting on an air of hospitality, getting busier in church and Bible study, or saying "sorry your feelings were hurt," which is just sugarcoated pretense. Underneath all of that is the root problem: we easily forget and distrust the love of God for us in Christ.

Misguided Rituals for Blessing

How many of us first volunteered for Great Commission service because we were projecting upon God an imperfect love? "God will love and bless me if I do hard things for him." "God will use me greatly and be proud of me if I sacrifice my life in his service among the unreached." And maybe once we have been in Great Commission service for a while, the spirituality we practice comes from the notion that our regular intimacy with God determines the blessings of God in our ministry. We might worry that the feelings aren't there anymore. And if the feelings are low, we are afraid our power is equally low.

As we inadvertently compare ourselves to others, we notice there seems to be the "haves" and the "have-nots." It can feel like God has made some super saints to be hotrods, always fast and flashy. We worry that there's something wrong with us when we cannot keep up. But it could be that God has just designed some of us to be semi-trucks, slowly hauling heavy loads. And others he made to be military vehicles, destroying enemy targets and getting attacked at the same time. While others are merely family sedans.

We tend to think that we must do something to keep the blessings flowing. For some, this might consist of getting away on spiritual retreats or conferences to reconnect with God again. It can feel like a high school church camp for more mature Great Commission servants—a few days to work up a spiritual high in order to re-engage the fray of ministry. Spiritual retreats aren't bad; I have found them beneficial. But they are false advertising when we interpret them as the source of our spiritual strength and endurance. The problem is when we fear diminishing power and blessing because we don't experience life-giving intimacy with God. So, some of us put our trust in "getting away from it all" instead of our union with Christ. Conferences and retreats can become rituals of getting back into God's blessing.

Many godly leaders speak extravagantly about soaking in God's mystical voice to tell us what he wants next or what he likes about us. If we're honest, the little impressions we feel are not terribly satisfying after a few days. They might give us a dopamine buzz for a weekend. But it disappears as soon as we get home to the city and face a thousand demands. We tend to put up pretenses because we are afraid that we either missed God's special voice or we have done something to quench the Spirit and mess everything up. And we go back to our weekly routine and operate with a mixture of guilt and shame. We hope that God is pleased and will bless our efforts eventually.

So much talk of the love of God in our ministry circles can consist of light devotions and simple songs about a potential subjective experience. That experience of God's love supposedly comes with enough sincerity, enough passion, and enough purity of heart. But after a few days of homeschooling, language study, commuting through the city, hours of emails, tedious expense reports, and dull administrative tasks, the anxiety of imperfect love comes back. God's perceived imperfect love is easily irritated. It feels like it frowns at us all day.

Yet, Great Commission spirituality that serves out of a stable, secure, glad-hearted contentment in union with Christ is such a happier alternative. It is far better than that up-and-down mystical spirituality that can be so unsettling. Immeasurably better. As those now severed from Adam's nature and growing into our new nature in Christ, what should be our daily response to God's love in Christ? To spurn our anxieties by remembering his promises. We grow spiritually as we receive and rest in God's promised love in Christ. We can live faithfully with a fearless, humble, hearty faith. Abiding in a prayerful communion with Christ is a life of humility.

Humble Hypocrites

I learned something about myself in my first few years of ministry: I was a hypocrite. I don't mean intentionally lying about what was true. That's just being a liar. The Greek word for hypocrite means *actor*. When Jesus chastises the religious leaders for hypocrisy, he is calling them posers, pretenders, performers.

To raise financial support in Great Commission service, we often feel like we can only talk about what our ministry partners are most interested in—what we are doing and how well we are doing. Occasionally, we can tell them when we are struggling, but it is easier to just mention our activities and accomplishments. If we are not careful, we might even project our own struggles upon those whom we are reaching and discipling. We might read into their lives what we are actually feeling. We become self-referential. Then people become ministry projects for us to fix.

I thank the Lord for giving me a few teachers and mentors in those early years who were models of both honesty and evangelical zeal.[7] Looking back, I realized that they were so devoted to the Great Commission because they had learned to receive God's love in their own lives. They had the honesty and humility to look into the dark places in their souls and deal with their junk. They found their security in their union with Christ and that compelled them to lay it all out. They could confess where they struggled and ask for help to grow in grace. They were not too ashamed or anxious to deal with their corrupt nature from Adam.

I was compelled to follow their example. Not because they were such amazing men, but because they turned away from the old Adam and pointed me to admire the new Adam in whose likeness they were becoming. I sensed a security with them. They modeled a tender peacefulness in Christ's love. Moments of admitting my struggles, confessing my sins, and remembering God's forgiveness in Christ were like retasting the sweetness of my conversion.

As we grow in humility and confidence in our union with Christ, we will know ourselves better for who we are in Christ despite the old Adamic nature that clings to us till our last breath. There are two poles on the spectrum of self-knowledge: an others-centered way and a self-centered way. The others-centered way acquires self-knowledge to learn where to be watchful for sinful tendencies. It helps us know how to pray for the love of God to chase out our insecurities and fears. It is rooted in a desire to honestly know where our fears hold us captive in order to anticipate that God's love will free us in those places.

---

7 I think of those years spent alongside my friend and mentor, John Gates, in personal evangelism in a closed country. He showed me how to love people with the truth. He exuded a spirit of compassionate honesty and genuine kindness that I've always wished to emulate. John taught me to humbly see people as they are and as they could be if redeemed in Christ. I also remember those evenings in my graduate school years, spent with my professor and mentor, Jerry Root. We would go out together often to practice personal evangelism on college campuses. His discipleship and C. S. Lewis-like influence were foundational for my understanding of humility and honesty in evangelism. Jerry taught me how to marvel at God's world as a Narnian and how to embrace humility and to witness with honesty. My supervisor and mentor, Lyle Dorsett, also invested into me personally and showed me how to pray, preach, and wait upon God to save souls. Lyle taught me how to serve with the power of the word and to humbly depend on the Holy Spirit for the salvation of souls. Much of this chapter is the fruit of adopting and integrating their teaching and intentional investment in my life.

The self-centered way of self-knowledge looks pious at first. But its navel-gazing can quickly spiral into self-preservation and self-vindication. It goes by the guise of, "preparing for ministry," "playing to our strengths," or "embracing weakness." It seems to frequently defer to the latest personality test, temperament review, and strength-mix survey *ad nauseum*. These can become slippery slopes to narcissism if we aren't careful.

We think knowing ourselves means being reminded of the features that we know about ourselves and that others know about us. This is where most of us focus on in our ministry—the public projection: "he's a powerful preacher," "she's a cheerful hostess," "he's a talented linguist," "she's so merciful and life-giving." People see these traits in us, and we see them in ourselves. This kind of affirmation helps boost our confidence in how God uses us functionally. But it is not as helpful for building us virtuously.

Humility and Virtue

There are also those areas of our lives that others see in us, but we don't see. This is like having bad breath or food stuck in our teeth that others notice, but we don't. Humility helps us listen when people kindly point out these unlovely features. We should want to know the truth about us that others see that we don't see. Having the humility to let our guard down and listen to others is essential for maintaining a right estimation of ourselves (bad breath and all). If we refuse to be honest about our blind spots, we will become defensive and self-referential. We will project our struggles onto others and treat people in a utilitarian way—using them to feel good about how successful or effective we are.

The humility to let others point out the patterns of faults in our lives that we don't see is the beginning of growth and learning. It is the beginning of maturity in other virtues. And if we respond rightly, our honesty about our sinful patterns and unsanctified personalities motivates other virtues to grow. True self-awareness, in the sanctified sense (not the psycho-babble sense), should lead to self-forgetfulness. False self-awareness leads to defensiveness. Learning from the good, bad, and ugly influences on our lives and being honest about our own good, bad, and ugly features gives us the humility to remember God's love in Christ. It helps us take down our defenses.

When humility cracks open our protective shell, we can show kindness, forbearance, and patience to one another because God does the same for us. We know how good forgiveness feels. As we serve in difficult fields with diverse people, the pressure-cooker of cross-cultural service can make us vent quite often. Remembering God's love in our union with Christ helps us see that God is patient and kind when we don't get it all right; we can extend the same latitude to others when they struggle. Adoniram Judson explained how security in God's love influences our self-forgetfulness and humility: "All true virtue has its root in the love of God. Every holy affection looks beyond self . . . and finds its resting place in God alone."[8]

The more we rest in our identity in Christ and God's perfect love for us, the more we realize how normal it is to battle sin. That realization should not encourage or excuse sin so that God's grace would abound. This is not permission to concede all manner of perverse sin and worldly vice. But we can rest assured that God expects us to undergo temptation and even to sin. But in union with Christ, we have direct access to our Father who is eager to grant us mercy and grace when we are struggling. He expects us to struggle. He is not angry with us for having weaknesses. We don't need to prove ourselves to him. That's why he united us to Christ as our High Priest:

> For we do not have a high priest who is unable to sympathize with our weaknesses, but one who in every respect has been tempted as we are, yet without sin. Let us then with confidence draw near to the throne of grace, that we may receive mercy and find grace to help in time of need. (Heb 4:15–16)

Humility sets us free from vice and frees us to grow in virtue. Once we cast off the vices of self-discovery, self-expression, and self-preservation, we can enjoy the freedom to be honest with a right assessment about who we are and who we are not. When we learn to meditate on God's love for us, we can have the humility, freedom, and courage to love like him. The Bible says, "We love because he first loved us" (1 John 4:19). God's love must shine his transforming grace upon us first before we can reflect it to others. Since pride disbelieves God's love, it takes humility to believe and receive God's love.

---

8 Burns, *Supreme Desire*, 174.

Humility and Christ's Work in Each of Us

The longer we serve in the Great Commission, the more we realize we are not all that important. We realize we contribute nothing of significance in and of ourselves. We should communicate and serve in a way that less would be said about us and more about Christ. Our job is to be like the pole that Moses used to lift up the bronze serpent in the wilderness. They looked to the cursed serpent and were healed (Num 21:8–9). If people look *at* us, let's make sure they do not look *to* us. Our job is to lift up Christ so that he is remembered and we are not. He must increase; we must decrease.

Paul instructs Timothy to "do your best to present yourself to God as one approved" (2 Tim 2:15). He doesn't say, be the best—just *do* your best. God grants each of us a measure of grace and faith to serve him in Christ:

> For by the grace given to me I say to everyone among you not to think of himself more highly than he ought to think, but to think with sober judgment, each according to the measure of faith that God has assigned. … Having gifts that differ accordingly to the grace given to us, let us use them; if prophecy, in proportion to our faith. (Rom 12:3, 6; see also 1 Cor 3:10)

Many reserve unswerving admiration for the most renowned and influential among us—those missionaries who have planted a dozen churches, those professors who keep publishing the most ground-breaking books, those pastors who command a following of thousands, those social media influencers who create cutting-edge missional content, those relief workers who rescue hundreds of kids from trafficking every year. But these are all just ordinary people. They get pimples, their worn clothes smell, they need to shower, their breath stinks in the morning, they get indigestion, they snore, and they get irritable and impatient. They're merely people.

We need to come to grips with the fact that we will just be another "begat." Like the list of genealogies recording who begat whom in the Old Testament, very few people will ever know our stories. Even fewer will choose to remember them. Every gravestone eventually goes unvisited. Even if one of us is regarded as "successful" and "famous" in a future generation, there will likely be a handful of young PhD candidates writing dissertations to show why our lives and works were partially right and mostly wrong. Every future generation thinks they know better, including our own. We are all suckers for blind "chronological snobbery," as Lewis would say.

We would benefit from reflecting occasionally on who has a higher regard for us—those who know us best (our family and close friends) or those who know us least (fans, followers, students, and church members). When we have gone to heaven, how will people remember us after a few years once the grief fades to only a dull ache?

The popular seventeenth-century preacher and chaplain of Oliver Cromwell's army, Thomas Fuller, meditated on the genealogy of good and bad kings in 2 Chronicles. Fuller contemplated his own good, fair, and poor influence on his son. His reflections were so tender and honest. I long to have a humble heart like this—giving thanks for my father's godly influences on me and hoping that my sinful influence on my own sons will not be perpetuated:

> Lord, I find the genealogy of my Savior strangely checkered with four remarkable changes in four immediate generations. (1) Rehoboam begat Abijah; that is, a bad father begat a bad son. (2) Abijah begat Asa; that is, a bad father begat a good son. (3) Asa begat Jehoshaphat; that is, a good father a good son. (4) Jehoshaphat begat Joram; that is, a good father a bad son. I see, Lord, from hence that my father's piety cannot be entailed [that is, generated in me]; that is bad news for me. But I see also that actual impiety is not always hereditary; that is good news for my son.[9]

Let us think of ourselves (and others) not too highly, but with a right and honest estimation—including historical heroes. Yes, give honor where honor is due, but don't overstate the case. Remember, God always has the last word. In our finite condition, we value someone's worth by their face, their place, and their race. But God looks upon the heart with grace. And all our rewards in the age to come are rewards of grace—Christ at work in us, through us, for us, to the glory of the grace of our Triune God.

It seems that every major strength has a corresponding struggle. Even the best of men are men at best. We all have clay feet, as it were. Some who excel in preaching, still struggle in counseling. Some who thrive in the prayer closet can be the most irritable in the deacon's meeting.

---

9 Elliot, *Keep a Quiet Heart*, 229; Wirt, ed., *Spiritual Disciplines*, 31.

A husband who spends his life providing for his family's earthly needs might struggle with basic soul care. A mother might be a sweet hostess but struggle with gossip.

We must not make excuses for perpetual weaknesses, flaws, and imperfections. Understanding our contexts can help us see who we are, why we struggle, and ways to address the issues. But we still have no excuse. We don't get a pass. The good news is that we are sinners justified through faith alone in union with Christ—*simul justus et peccator*. We are not justified by our add-ons and adverbs: faithful enough, sincerity of heart, radical obedience, sold out commitment, total surrender, abandoned devotion, crazy reckless love, etc. Our enoughness is never enough.

As we pursue Great Commission spirituality, it helps to contemplate our historical "heroes" and even ourselves in an honest context. We can discuss their flaws, and acknowledge our own, with confidence that we have all died with Christ and have been raised with him. The Great Commission life we now live is Christ in us, through us, and in spite of us.

By recognizing this truth, we can maintain an honest perspective on our own strengths and weakness. And by extension, we can entertain honest estimations of others too. We are not all weak and broken. Despite the victim-mindset of recent years, brokenness and weakness are not humility. We will be perfectly humble in heaven as virtuous saints, but neither broken nor weak. In this life, godly grief and contrition might serve our virtue, but in heaven, grief and contrition will be as far from us as the east is from the west. Since the Bride will see her Bridegroom face to face in love, naked and unashamed as it were, then honesty and humility will remain.

Weakness, grief, and brokenness are not virtues. Therefore, though strength, endurance, and courage might be perceived as self-confidence and arrogance, they are not contrary to virtue. They do not oppose humility. We can be simultaneously courageous and humble. Jesus is a lion and a lamb—both merciful and mighty, humble and strong. God indeed makes us strong and courageous, even in horrific weakness and affliction. To be sure, God causes us to conquer. In fact, we are more than conquerors. How? Through the love the Triune God has for us in our union with Christ:

> Who shall separate us from the love of Christ? Shall tribulation, or distress, or persecution, or famine, or nakedness, or danger, or sword? As it is written,
>
> "For your sake we are being killed all the day long;
> we are regarded as sheep to be slaughtered."
>
> No, in all these things we are more than conquerors through him who loved us. For I am sure that neither death nor life, nor angels nor rulers, nor things present nor things to come, nor powers, nor height nor depth, nor anything else in all creation, will be able to separate us from the love of God in Christ Jesus our Lord. (Rom 8:35–39)

Humility and Honesty in Witness

One of the most debilitating hurdles to telling others the gospel message is that we have lost a sense of how amazing God's grace is in our own lives. We may seek to bring the gospel light into the lives of others, but we often neglect to keep its light burning in our own lives. One of the best things we can do to revive a commitment to witness is to be re-converted every day to the love of God in Christ. I am writing this book for this reason—to refresh us in the love of God in our union with Christ, and to propel us to serve faithfully in the Great Commission.

As the Lord sanctified me and brought me face to face with the residue of sin in my soul, my approach to witnessing changed. The honest acknowledgement of my ongoing sin nature and imperfection in light of Christ's abiding love transformed my gospel conversations with unbelievers.

In the past, I focused mainly on the clarity and accuracy of the content, which is right and good. No apologies for that whatsoever. However, often I wondered how I could avoid any perceived pretense in my presentation. It's one thing if the gospel is offensive; it's another if my manner or approach is offensive. I didn't intend to sound like a strait-laced religious simpleton. But we all know that perception is reality. And I was fully aware of how easy it is to project our previous experiences onto others. I assumed that my conversation partner (friend, student, taxi driver, etc.) was likely projecting onto me what they thought was true of religious people or Americans or whatever category they had placed me in.

So, I started explaining the good news through an autobiographical filter. I do not mean that I recalled the account of my conversion and how much better my life is now—what we tend to think of when we hear the word "testimony." I mean I spoke of my dire need for a Savior and how God's grace in Christ met and continues to meet me in those hard-to-reach places. I was general enough to name the struggle or sin, but not too specific to tempt them to voyeurism.

When I learned to talk in an honest manner (not a trite, victimized, defeatist way) about how I struggled with anger, pride, discontentment, depression, and the like, I found the person would listen intently. Maybe they had never heard anyone attempt to be honest and open before. In some of the cultures where I have served for the last twenty years, confession of sin and openness about weakness are never practiced. Christians and even pastors in those cultures rarely, if ever, confess sin. It's shameful. Even more so those for who have yet to be born again.

Think of how a novel's character development draws us in and marshals our imagination to see through the character's eyes. Similarly, telling genuine stories of redemption from our own lives draws people in like a documentary. It helps them heed the threads and themes of grace and God's love in Christ. I wanted to tell the news of Christ, his work of redemption, and how his work satisfied my own honest need for redemption. Learning to do so enabled me to naturally transition to their own life stories. I wanted to draw out those patterns and places that point them to their need for redemption.

I would learn to ask fairly impersonal and common questions like, "Where do you call home?" "What do you love to do?" "How is your family?" Every answer is an open door to walk through with another more personal question. If they call Damascus home, but we are in Istanbul, I might follow up with a comment that expressed a level of perceptiveness or care: "Wow, that must be hard driving taxi in a country that doesn't speak your language" (since Turks don't speak Arabic). To which they might respond, "It's not bad, but my family has been stuck in Syria ever since the war."

They just gave me permission to walk through another, more private door that is touching something sensitive in their soul. Maybe they want to go there now, maybe they do not. But either way, Jesus can go there. My job is to nudge them toward Christ, one step at a time. Then, depending on the situation and more back-and-forth, I might say, "Has anyone ever told you how sad it is that your family has suffered such devastation? I am truly sorry." The conversation might end there with a cool emotional silence. Or it might go on. I have learned to not worry too much about wrapping up the conversation with a gospel presentation. I initially try to witness to Christ's power in me to work through me. I try to use simple, honest statements about my struggles, my attempts and corresponding failures to fix my sin by myself, and how kind God is in Christ to save my soul and empower me to grow closer to Christ.

But, if I could, how would I transition into the gospel? In a conversation like the one above, I casually let them know I am a Christian. I am a professor who teaches the Bible and Christian history. I tell them that the God of the Bible promises to hear and draw near to his people when they pray. I offer to pray for that person. In all my life, in every city, country, and village I have been in, only twice can I remember my offer to pray being rejected. In one of those instances, I was talking to a witch who was likely demonically oppressed. The other time I observed that the person was carrying genuine conviction of some secret sin and was terrified of God.

When I offer to pray for someone, either I do it there if it seems socially appropriate, or I do it later that day. Do I always explain the four common features of a gospel presentation (God, Man, Christ, Response)? Not always. I do ask, though, if they have ever met a Christian before. And I ask if anyone has ever clearly explained the gospel to them. It doesn't always work that way, but sometimes, when I don't expect it, the Spirit of God makes a way. He helps me to clearly explain the gospel and the love of God in Christ. It never hurts to ask. Sometimes the conversation leads to multiple meetings where I can teach them the story of redemption.

I remember speaking with one man whose defenses were up because of past religious abuse. He was throwing around the word "hypocrite" like a curse word. I said to him, "I don't know what you have had to suffer in the past. Even if I did know, I would not understand how bad it was. But I can tell you this, I am one of those hypocrites too. I teach others about the love of God, but I have always struggled to love people as much as I love myself. I preach about the grace of God's forgiveness, but I have been slow to forgive some who have wronged me. Though God is the perfect Father, I am aware every day of how flawed I am as a father. Yes, I am an actor like a hypocrite—I put on a mask and pretend I'm someone else. Sometimes I don't want people to know how rotten I feel. I walk into church happy to see people when I was just irritated with my boys a few minutes before in the car. But one thing I do know is that God loves to save bad people. And I am so thankful that he shows his love for me in that while I was and am still a sinner, Christ died for me." That man did not convert to Christ in my presence that day. But he was visibly jolted by the hopefulness that he too could be a forgiven sinner, a struggler whom God loves nevertheless.

That is the power of a regular contemplation of our union in Christ and how it informs and influences our witness. We can never love people enough. Only God can. So, when we witness the truth in love, we can only tell the truth in a sufficiently loving way if the love we hold out is God's love (not merely our expressed love). Yes, we should witness in a loving manner. But unbelievers should not be impressed with our loving demeanor and kind-sounding words as much as God's love for sinners in Christ.

This approach to a gospel conversation nullifies any blind accusation of hypocrisy and self-righteous pretension they might have toward Christians (or religious people). The authenticity of humility and honesty can catch them by surprise. In cultures that esteem saving face even by deception and lying, we might be the first genuinely honest person they have talked to in a very long time.

People from these cultures often have an unsettling fascination with self-effacing honesty. It unmasks an attractive personal security that they cannot compute. The mask is off. The face is seen, warts and all. And though our metaphorical face is less than ideal and asymmetrical with its blemishes, we're not terribly ashamed. Why is that? Because our security and identity are in Christ, who is the face of God. Honesty is not weakness; it is the fruit of security and assurance in God's love for us in Christ. So, let's be honest. Let's talk about our struggles. Let's never be afraid to give others the convicting and comforting word of Christ about the complete work of Christ.

Humility to Not Be in Control

When someone is learning to drive, one of the initial temptations is to watch the sides of the road or oncoming traffic so carefully that the new driver drives into the ditch or into traffic. But God has given us peripheral vision to mind the ditches and to look straight ahead. By focusing on the road, we can remain watchful and still avoid threats outside our lane. An inordinate and unhealthy focus on self-knowledge as discussed above can lead us to drive into the ditches of sin—always thinking about lust, discontentment, or anxiety in the name of fighting against those temptations. Maintaining an honest estimation of the good, bad, and ugly of our souls helps us remember where the ditches are without focusing. We should focus on Jesus and our united participation in him and his life.

This kind of humility should lead to courageously keeping the word, even when it feels impractical or ineffective. Paul could have appealed to multiple spectacular heavenly experiences with Christ as an argument for his missionary calling. But, instead of impressing people with his visions, he appealed to Scripture as the ground of his ambition:

> Thus I make it my ambition to preach the gospel, not where Christ has already been named, lest I build on someone else's foundation, *but as it is written*,
>
> > "Those who have never been told of him will see,
> > and those who have never heard will understand."
>
> (Rom 15:20–21; emphasis added)

Paul endeavored "not to go beyond what is written" (1 Cor 4:6) in defending or commending the ministry God had commanded him.

We must have the courage to abide so closely in the word of Christ, teaching all of it (even its hard, politically incorrect, and counter-cultural truths) at every opportunity we get. We must have the humility to watch out for our propensity to innovate the word and get creative beyond what is written. In Isaiah's day, some got desperate for a new "word" from the Lord, so they asked spiritists to listen for God's voice. But God refused to indulge them. He warned that if they did not listen to his Scripture, they would have no light and wander about distressed:

> And when they say to you, "Inquire of the mediums and the necromancers who chirp and mutter," should not a people inquire of their God? Should they inquire of the dead on behalf of the living? To the teaching and to the testimony! If they will not speak according to this word, it is because they have no dawn. They will pass through the land, greatly distressed and hungry. (Isa 8:19–21)

To extend the driving analogy above, if we are driving around a mountain or a plateau, we might get bored and try driving off-road and over the terrain. We may still get to our destination, but we may not. If we do, our vehicle will likely be in a battered condition. But if we drive on the road and keep within the lines, we should get to our destination in a timely manner. Similarly, God will empower what he has commanded. But he might or might not empower what we innovate. And he might or might not empower anything he has not clearly commanded.

The patriarchs in Genesis tried to manufacture the promises in their own way, and God stymied their efforts. God was still faithful to his promise, but in his way. God has given us promises, and he has given us commands in light of those promises (e.g., the Great Commission). He will empower our obedience to his commands. If he commands it, he empowers it. But if we try to control the fruit-bearing process and make imperatives out of biblical implications, then we are in danger of trying to accomplish something apart from God's power. Our extra biblical methods of spirituality and service will likely be unfruitful and ineffective in the long run.

Like Jehoshaphat, when he was surrounded by enemies, our response should be very humble: "O our God, will you not execute judgment on them? For we are powerless against this great horde that is coming against us. We do not know what to do, but our eyes are on you" (2 Chr 20:12). Essentially, the cry of humility is, "Lord, I know what you have promised. I am overwhelmed and helpless. I don't know what to do, but my eyes are on you."

Organic Cultivation or Innovative Production?

Wendell Berry contrasts modern farming and animal husbandry in *The Unsettling of America*. He speaks of the modern desire to meet the bottom line with farming and how it has ruined the soil, the animals, and the actual produce. He contrasts the mindset of a farmer of a small plot of land to the mindset of a coal producer. Those who produce coal and other mining elements focus on the profit based upon the amount they can extract. They devastate the land in the process. But animal husbandry and farming focus on creating an environment where the farmer is not in control of production. The farmer simply facilitates an organic, healthy, and rich environment where the plants and animals can receive nourishment and thrive accordingly. Health naturally produces fruit. A healthy apple tree produces apples because that is its identity. The farmer cannot force or control its life and growth. Berry says, "The damages of our present agriculture all come from the determination to use the life of the soil as if it were an extractable resource like coal, to use living things as if they were machines, to impose scientific (that is, laboratory) exactitude upon living complexities that are ultimately mysterious."[10]

Contemplating God's creation in Christ helps us see into the analogies of life. I live in the jungled mountains of Southeast Asia, where fruit trees grow wild all year. We can pick fruit on our mountain property any time, but the fruit is not always ripe. Most fruit is hard and sour for a long time before it turns soft and sweet. Only the combination of rain, sun, and time enables fruit trees to bear good fruit. So it is with all of us. Through a combination of heat, storms, and time under the providence of Christ's good care, we bear fruit and so prove to be his disciples. Until then, let us be humble and patient with the hardness and sourness of our lives and the lives of those around us. Christ will soften and sweeten us in time. We must have the humility, like a farmer, to cultivate a healthy environment where souls can hear the teachings of the love of God and grow steadily in that love, season by season.

If we are secure and confident in our loving union with Christ, we will spend ourselves humbly in his service according to his word. We will not vie for first place. We will be content to deflect attention away from ourselves and point people to Christ, his truth, and his love. We are not the point. We don't need to worry about manufacturing a fruit-bearing production line. We don't need to be in control. It never works out well. Our manufactured fruit is always cheap, artificial, and tasteless.

True love brings the object of its love to the source of all love—Jesus Christ. As we grow in love for Christ, we fall out of love with ourselves. Our Great Commission service takes on a new flavor—people increasingly remember Jesus more than us. May our Great Commission spirituality be so tethered in union with Christ that they see more of him and less of us.

Just as in Dante's *Paradiso*, his true love, Beatrice (symbolizing theology and piety), directs Dante's "longing to its goal"[11] in heaven as he approaches

10 Berry, *Unsettling of America*, 94.

11 Dante, *Paradiso*, 402

the Beatific Vision. He sees her but she looks away from him. She looks instead to the face of God in Christ. She points Dante to his *telos*: Beatrice "smiled and looked down at me, then turned again to the eternal fountain."[12] May we be humble enough to not attempt to control production. Instead, let's create an *evangel*-environment that influences souls in the way of Christ, with the word of Christ, to rest in union with Christ.

A Prayerful Instinct of Abiding with Humility in Christ

Isn't it amazing how this theme of union with Christ is so pervasive and practical for the grind of gospel service? God does indeed strengthen and empower us for his tasks and assignments in Christ. Humility is honest about those times and occasions when God seems to use our efforts in great ways. False humility would downplay it as nothing. Humility is unphased by what others say about us—both the flatterers and the accusers. Humility is suspicious of its own press. Nevertheless, humility listens to what others say, but heeds finally what God says.

This constant instinct to abide in God's grace in Christ saves us from both depressive introspection and inflated self-confidence. Humility serves our Great Commission spirituality because it creates a home of quietness before the Lord where we can rest and know that the Father always receives us, forgives us, listens to us, and helps us. Since perfect love casts out fear, and peace is the alternative to fear, humility and peace are closely connected. Where there is a maturing virtue of humility, there will be an ever-present sense of peace in God. We will enjoy glad-hearted contentment in God that says, "Jesus is enough for me."

Though our best is never good enough, our union with Christ ensures that God always receives our service as a thank offering through our faith in Christ. God remembers and will reward the work of Christ in us and through us. We can anticipate that we will face temptation and sin. God is not surprised. Neither should we be surprised. We are all saints with bad pasts and sinners with good futures. He has made a way out in those times of need and weakness. Prayerfully contemplating and remembering our union with Christ will free us to be self-forgetful out of love for those whom Jesus brings into our lives.

---

12 Dante, 404

Humility is perfect quietness of heart. It is to expect nothing, to wonder at nothing that is done to me, to feel nothing done against me. It is to be at rest when nobody praises me, and when I am blamed or despised. It is to have a blessed home in the Lord, where I can go in and shut the door, and kneel to my Father in secret, and am at peace as in a deep sea of calmness, when all around and above is trouble.

—Andrew Murray

Chapter 7 Courage

Abiding in Christ When All We Have Is Christ

Scripture for Meditation

Be of good courage, and let us be courageous for our people, and for the cities of our God, and may the Lord do what seems good to him.

—2 Samuel 10:12

Many have lionized Martin Luther for his smart quip that he and his partners merely preached the word, drank Wittenberg beer, and watched God's word fuel the Reformation:

> I simply taught, preached, and wrote God's Word; otherwise I did nothing. And while I slept, or drank Wittenberg beer with my friends Philipp and Amsdorf, the Word so greatly weakened the papacy that no prince or emperor ever inflicted such losses upon it. I did nothing; the Word did everything.[1]

Those who uphold the authority and sufficiency of the written word love this quote. And I do too. It truly champions the essence of the power of God's written word. Yet, after formally studying church history and

1 Bainton, *Here I Stand*, 212; see Luther, *Sermons 1*, 77.

teaching it myself in seminary, I have learned to read Christian leaders like Luther in their own personal and historical context as much as possible.

Luther made that famous remark in 1522—five years after he nailed his famous 95 theses on the Wittenberg church door, effectively launching the Protestant Reformation. From 1517 to 1525, Luther was a firebrand. He demolished every argument raised up against the knowledge of Christ. He was doing the work of a missionary—translating the Bible into German (from the original languages rather than the Latin Vulgate). He was also doing the work of a reformer—teaching the Bible alone to a nominal, culturally Christian, Roman Catholic populace who had never heard the Bible in their native tongue. During those initial years, Luther experienced the drama, adventure, action, romance, and suspense of seeing Christ build his church throughout the Germanic region.

We rightly celebrate Luther for defying the papacy and unbiblical Roman Catholic dogma and traditions. But we forget that it took equal courage to press on when the extraordinary fires of renewal had dwindled. Luther needed an uncommon endurance to shepherd the remaining poor, ordinary folk who needed to mature in basic faith and love. After 1525 and the end of the Peasants' War, the rapid gospel-spreading movement had slowed from a mighty flood to a modest stream. Luther himself struggled with chronic health issues related to aging and years of stress. And he was becoming increasingly aware that the anticipated return of Christ might not be as immediate as he had envisioned.

The progress of the kingdom never ceased, but it sure seemed like it lost the momentum of the glory days right after 1517. So much for perpetual lay-led, rapid-cycle church-planting movements. Luther felt disillusioned with rampant antinomianism, disunity, and bickering among the parishioners. He suffered the drain of incessant theological controversy and argumentation, the emperor's disapproval of the Augsburg Confession, and the Jews' refusal to convert to Christ.

Luther realized he would need the courage to endure for a long life of routine discipleship, church order, and pastoral care. The sweetness of abiding in Christ, maturing in that union, and teaching families to enjoy their life in Christ became Luther's mainstay. That was his table talk. He had to cultivate the humility and the courage to see the extraordinary in the ordinary.

Indeed, Luther had to come to terms with the fact that the work would still exist generations after him. It would be a bitter struggle till Christ returns. He had no categories for any sort of triumphalist Christianization of the world to usher in the return of Christ. Luther had to learn to rest in Christ as his life. Luther confessed that Christ is the King of his kingdom. He alone builds his church. We may be ambassadors of the King, but we don't build his kingdom.

Life to the Hilt in Christ

In this final chapter, I am writing straightforwardly to stir up the coals of our union with Christ. May the Lord fan them into a flame of boldness that lives by hearty faith in the promises of God. Though the task is intimidating and fearful, the promises are exceedingly greater. Those promises are all yes and amen in Christ. Let us live life to the hilt by faith in our union with Christ. Let us race across the finish line with our veins bulging. This chapter will be the most personal for me because of how much courage and endurance the Lord has had to give me for his mysterious providences.

For eleven years I directed a Master of Arts program in global leadership (or Great Commission leadership) at an American seminary. If anyone would observe the books on my shelves, they would be hard-pressed to find books on leadership. Most popular books on leadership I've read seem to highlight managing measurable points of progress, production, and profit. I don't typically study books on leadership; I prefer to study men of courage. I read biographies and listen to people whose courage was contagious. The people under their influence felt compelled to follow their lead not because they were "leaders." They followed because they observed a combination of courage, passion, and endurance in one purposeful direction that inspired them. They contended with a boldness that commanded loyalty and captured the hearts of their peers.

The legendary heroes of the church whom we honor today were no pushovers. Besides the fact that they were all flawed, the one virtue that stands out in every prominent case is their boldness. Among their number were pastors and farmers, Europeans and Africans, the self-taught and the scholars, the healthy and the chronically ill. But in every case, their courage in Christ drove them to bear fruit for generations. They proclaimed God's love in truth and God's truth in love. Theirs was an unswerving allegiance to the written word. They endured, against all odds, in hope of God's promises.

Such courage in Great Commission service never comes from personality or raw willpower. It cannot. Great Commission service is a supernatural work. It demands speaking the word to valleys of dry bones and watching God give them life. Though it is a supernatural and miraculous work, it demands courage, nonetheless. In Great Commission spirituality, abiding prayerfully in our union with Christ is how we derive hope to endure with courage. The Bible says that "in [Christ] we have boldness and access with confidence through our faith in him" (Eph 3:12). Because of the glory of our ministry of righteousness in Christ, still yet to be revealed in full, Paul says, "since we have such a hope, we are very bold" (2 Cor 3:12).

Courage and Cowardice

An epidemic of cowardice has weakened many hearts in recent years. With the ubiquity of social media and our continual peering into picture-perfect, happy lives, the fear of missing out on God's best is hindering us from taking responsibility for the gospel among the nations. We limit ourselves to our personality profile and basically tell God what kind of ministry positions we could do best. After all, we assure ourselves, God would never give us anything more than we can handle.

The reality is that standing alone on the truth always seems like more than anyone can handle. We often fear standing alone and doing what is right by God's word. The courage to lead with the truth, and all its sharp edges, is never a popular virtue. The theologian John Murray offered a timeless admonition to those called to lead courageously with the word:

> You will be tempted to soften the stroke and to modify the truth. Remember in this hour of temptation—a temptation made doubly plausible by what appears to be consideration for the feelings of your people—remember the terms of the divine commission, 'to *all* that I shall send thee, *whatsoever* I command thee, thou shalt speak.' And take your comfort from the remembrance that one day the pure and undimmed light of him who has commissioned you will descend not only upon the panorama of observable history but upon the hearts and secret lives of all men.[2]

2 Murray, *Collected Writings*, 176–77. Emphasis in original.

Great Commission service commands an in-your-face kind of boldness. It stares vice, controversy, and social shame in the face and refuses to yield in submission even for a moment (Gal 2:5). No compromise. This level of commitment requires a spirituality fortified by the abiding presence of Christ. We can stand alone as not alone. The righteous are bold as a lion (Prov 28:1). That is only true because of our vital union with the Lion of Judah. His boldness surges within us, behind us, and for us. As Hudson Taylor would claim, "What are lions' dens when the Lion of the tribe of Judah is with us?"[3] Paul rehearsed it this way: "If God is for us, who can be against us" (Rom 8:31). Note the preposition: *for*—not just *with*. God is *for* us. When infinite omnipotence, omniscience, and omnipresence are devoted to defend us, preserve us, and strengthen us, who or what can ever succeed against us?

Such promises ensure that Christians have no reason to let fear rule them. To occasionally struggle with fear is to be expected, which is why we have so many great assurances of God's abiding presence in Christ. But letting ungodly fear rule our souls is not a Christian trait. Cowardice is a vice, not a virtue. Since the righteous are as bold as a lion, the unrighteous, in contrast, are marked by cowardice.

It's fascinating to notice the list of the eight vices thrown into the lake of fire in Revelation 21:8. What vice is the first to be cast into the lake of fire? Cowardice. The verse right before it commends those who boldly conquer as the heirs and inheritance of God. Cowardice abides in fear apart from the love of God. Those who conquer and endure to the end in Revelation are anything but cowardly. As we shall see in the next section, if courage is among the highest virtues, then cowardice is among the lowest vices.

Warriors, Poets, and Jesters

We love courage instinctively. Most of our stories are about courage. Every standard drama has a conflict, rising action, climax, and resolution. At the point of climax courage is tested and proven to be unbreakable. What is it about courage that is so awe-inspiring? It does something uncommon. Courage acts on a promise unseen, in a way that proves its authenticity. Beauty and mystery might fade or prove to be empty. But courage inspires us to a higher level of awe and reverence. Courage looks

3 Taylor, *Union and Communion*, 52.

like an otherworldly virtue because it demands that faith, hope, and love work in tandem for something or someone beyond our normal senses. It acts upon a promise. It puts everything on the line. It never looks back. It burns the ships and leads into the dark unknown.

There are three kinds of men in every age: The jesters, who perform or listen to music, the poets, who write that music, and the warriors, who inspire the poets. Power and glory inspire men to make music. And what makes power and glory music-worthy? When courage that forges powerful and glorious men is tested and proven genuine. The steel of a sword is heat-treated and beaten to become both hard and shiny. The sword becomes powerful and glorious, strong and beautiful. The crucible demands courage for the soul to endure. In the crucible, all the fires of hell, the shadow of death's impenetrable gloom, and the crushing weight of the world are hammering the soul. While our metal is in the fire and under pressure, the steel of the soul mysteriously transforms into a sword. Once the blade emerges from its refinement, it reveals a convergence of strength and beauty. The artisan-blacksmith glories in his ornate warcraft.

Admittedly, this is a debatable assertion, but courage is described in the Bible as an inherently masculine attribute, just as nurture and nursing are inherently feminine attributes. It doesn't mean women are never courageous. In fact, women are among the most courageous Great Commission servants I have known, and history has recorded. Many women who reached lost souls and died brutal deaths on the mission field were courageous beyond their peers. The fact that most Great Commission servants around the world are single women should tell us something about their mettle. They are daughters of Sarah, those who "do good and do not fear anything that is frightening" (1 Pet 3:6).

In the Bible, commands to be courageous in both the Hebrew and the Greek literally say, "play the man" or "act like men" (2 Sam 10:12; 1 Cor 16:13). Contemporary versions typically translate as "be very courageous." Because of this manly attribution, biblical courage is associated with warfare imagery. To be sure, Scripture does not call the church to transgress its sphere and to take up the sword belonging to the king. Nevertheless, the mindset of a warrior is fitting for a Great Commission servant. To be a courageous soldier for Christ demands tenacity, self-denial, and allegiance to the honor of the King.

Consider the imagery of lion-like boldness in J. R. R. Tolkien's account of Aragorn leading his party to take the Paths of the Dead. They have exhausted their endurance. Even Gimli, the brave-hearted dwarf, feels at his limit. Tolkien describes Aragorn's determination to press on: "But when the dawn came, cold and pale, Aragorn rose at once, and led the Company forth upon the journey of greatest haste and weariness that any among them had ever known, save he alone, and only his will held them to go on."[4]

Those three words, "save he alone," are profound. He knew the path of pain and fear. Every step along the way in his journey was leading him to this point. Aragorn inspires the boldness his party needs to tread through the darkness. Moreover, he becomes the courage others need who have none of their own. Gimli says, "I was held to the road only by the will of Aragorn."[5] Without Aragorn's unflinching courage and kindhearted strength, fear would have dismantled the small company.

Many people want to keep their options open and have the flexibility to pivot to something or somewhere else when the heat is turned up. They are like jesters, making melody with the music of the poets, inspired by the warriors. Great Commission servants who are secure in their royal identity in a kingly bloodline, like Aragorn, exude hope, benevolence, and great-heartedness that the company sees as courage. That courage ennobles every other virtue as they plod on in their mission.

Courage and Virtue

As demonstrated in the previous chapter, honesty and humility are two sides of the same coin. We can't have one without the other. They are the building blocks of all other virtues. And if humility is the ground upon which and out of which all other virtues grow, then courage is the highest virtue in this life (where we still face threats and fear) before we are perfected in love in the resurrection. Courage requires humility. Humility requires courage. They are bookends to a volume of virtues. How so? The ancients always associated courage with the warrior; it is his highest, most excellent virtue. Courage is the supreme virtue because that is where all other virtues (like faith, hope, and love) are proven and verified as true.

4 Tolkien, *Return of the King*, 25, Kindle Edition, Location 979.

5 Tolkien, 71, Kindle Edition, Location 2652.

C. S. Lewis well said that "courage is not simply *one* of the virtues, but the form of every virtue at the testing point."[6] If our virtues give way to vice when we are under pressure, then we merely upheld virtue when conditions were convenient. Virtue that endures in trial requires unbreakable courage. Courage to persevere through testing proves our faith in God, our hope in his promises, and our affectionate devotion to him. Courage establishes those virtues God is hammering into us. It grows out of humility because it requires a devout affection and unswerving allegiance to what is true.

Both classical philosophy and Christian theology have taught similar versions of the cardinal virtues—four transculturally supreme virtues that inform ethical living. They are not exhaustive, but merely illustrative: wisdom, righteousness, courage, and self-control. Peter uses synonymous language and structures them in a way to show the heart of growing in virtue. As discussed in chapter 1, since God has promised future glorification to those in union with Christ (2 Pet 1:3–4), Peter responds with these precepts:

> For this very reason, make every effort to supplement your faith with virtue, and virtue with knowledge, and knowledge with self-control, and self-control with steadfastness, and steadfastness with godliness, and godliness with brotherly affection, and brotherly affection with love. (2 Pet 1:5–7)

In a chiastic structure, the very center virtue here would be steadfastness (i.e., endurance, fortitude). By placing steadfastness at the center, Peter is highlighting it as the main axis on which Christian virtues turn, from top to bottom, from faith to love. Steadfastness is the necessary offshoot of courage because it suggests there are fearful threats that tempt us to quit, but we courageously cling to the promises and therefore *stand fast.*

Lewis observed that "fortitude includes both kinds of courage—the kind that faces danger as well as the kind that 'sticks it' under pain. 'Guts' is perhaps the nearest modern English. You will notice, of course, that you cannot practice any of the other virtues very long without bringing this one into play."[7]

---

6 Lewis, *Screwtape Letters*, 161. Emphasis in original.

7 Lewis, *Mere Christianity*, 79.

Biblical history tells the stories of those who built their honor through years of virtue and then sullied their name in a foolish moment of vice. One cowardly minute of vice can unleash a lifetime of ongoing consequences. Moses, the humblest man who ever lived, had outbursts of anger that prevented him from entering the Promised Land. David, a man after God's own heart, lost his kingdom over adultery and murder. Solomon, the wisest man who ever lived, played the fool and succumbed to forbidden women, exhibiting a lack of self-control. Peter, the rock upon whom the Lord would build his church, denied Christ three times. Each of these people failed the final point of testing where fortitude was necessary to persevere in virtue.

What is the outcome for those who persevere courageously in the virtues of the Spirit? Peter says, "for if these qualities are yours and are increasing, they keep you from being ineffective or unfruitful in the knowledge of our Lord Jesus Christ" (2 Pet 1:8). Great Commission servants who remember the promises in Christ and courageously endure in view of those promises add to their spirituality virtues like love, piety, temperance, righteousness, wisdom, and self-control. In our Great Commission service, a life ever increasing in these virtues will not cease to be effective and fruitful.

Theologians of Glory and of the Cross

The instruments of our lives are so flawed that nothing is ever perfect or meritorious. Therefore, we need to be united to Christ for our service to be translated as pleasing to God. Anyone who has served for an honest hour in the Great Commission will attest to the defective nature of our minds, hearts, bodies, wills, and abilities. Luther acknowledged that all Christians do theology (whether or not we are formally trained) by making assertions and acting upon what we believe to be true about God, Man, Christ, and our reasonable response.

Though most of us would not claim the title of "theologian," we are all theologians in some measure. Luther gave a few distinctions to the two broad categories of possible theologians. In our maturation and spirituality, we are either theologians of glory or theologians of the cross: "He deserves to be called a theologian, however, who comprehends the visible and manifest things of God through suffering and the cross. A theologian of glory calls evil good and good evil. A theologian of the cross calls the thing what it actually is."[8]

---

8 Luther, *Luther's Works*, 40.

The theologian of glory makes the mistake of looking at how people in the world operate in order to discern who God must be. He assumes that the Trinity will function in the same way that our own human relationships operate. The theologian of glory takes note of *quid pro quo* business transactions and assumes that God will do us favors when we do good things for him. It's a kind of karmic Christianity. In contrast, instead of looking to creation and projecting the way things seem to work upon God, theologians of the cross start with Scripture and then see creation as analogies of life that echo biblical truths.

Theologians of glory look at the power of God as a kingly power—to coerce and demand allegiance. They look to God to do the miraculous outside of the ordinary means of grace and gospel growth. They look to Christ for the benefits of glory, as the distributer of the gifts they have always wanted. Jesus uses his power to repair us from the inside and helps us to be happy forever. It is an internal work of renovation through the assistance of grace.

However, theologians of the cross see power as demonstrated by the grace of God through weakness. And the greatest display of power was the cross itself. They look to Christ not primarily as the distributer of gifts or benefits, but as the gift himself. Christ himself is the *telos* of faith. Jesus alone is the exceedingly great reward for theologians of the cross. Jesus uses his power to redeem us from outside ourselves. He declares to us that we are united with him forever. It is an external work of new creation through the announcement of grace.

Theologians of glory consider righteousness to be marked by outward compliance to a code of conduct. They focus on refined decorum, honor, civility, and good behavior. In contrast, the theologian of the cross understands righteousness as the alien righteousness accounted to us by the God-honoring obedient Man on the cross.

Theologians of glory look at wisdom as the world practices it and assume it provides principles for success, the keys for prosperity, and how to maximize human flourishing. These applications of wisdom are all baptized in theological language, but they are pragmatic and worldly-wise at best. However, theologians of the cross see wisdom in its full manifestation when the Son of God himself hung naked and weak on a Roman cross.

The theologian of glory recoils at the thought of death and sees it only as the enemy of life. Death, suffering, and dying should be avoided at all costs. God's will is for our abundance, happiness, health, flourishing, and wholeness. Anything that opens itself to tribulation and adversity for the glory of God and the good of others is not God's desire for us. Alternatively, the theologian of the cross welcomes death and dying. This is not because death is good, but because it is the pathway to paradise and abundant life in Christ. Christ himself is the way, and in union with him, we can say with Paul: "I have been crucified with Christ. It is no longer I who live, but Christ who lives in me" (Gal 2:20). The way to heaven has been secured by his blood. Yet even in union with Christ we suffer along the way: We are "heirs of God and fellow heirs with Christ, provided we suffer with him in order that we may also be glorified with him" (Rom 8:17). Someday our dying will give way to immortality. His life in us through his death for us is the only way.

Courage to Limp

Theologians of glory are everywhere in Great Commission service. In a way, this whole book is written to push back against the damaging, discouraging advice of these peddlers of power. They mean well, of course, but good intentions are no excuse for bad counsel. Such theologians of glory imply that we can have true intimacy with Jesus, more than enough support, accessible visa platforms, family flourishing, and dynamic language skills, simply by imitating more fruitful Great Commission servants. They make assertions that God wouldn't want his servants to be strugglers. There's no place for chronic illness among God's MVPs. He wants us to be happy, healthy, and abounding in blessing. How so? Theologians of glory suggest we must employ tried-and-true methodologies and practice special spiritual disciplines. They advise that we wait for God to give us direct words for decision-making before we step outside his will. They offer other methods that they have either practiced and found successful or have heard successful reports from others.

This approach to ministry is just a soft prosperity gospel for strait-laced evangelicals. Those who promote such ideas have big hearts that love Jesus and want to make a difference in the world. They are others-centered, passionate, and devoted to a good cause. Yet, so much of their

Great Commission service is bound up in a fear of displeasing God, a fear of missing the direction of the Holy Spirit, a fear of quenching the Spirit, a fear of weakness that would slow down their progress, and a fear of fruitlessness. These common emotions and fears arise from years of imbibing the stories and suggestions of theologians of glory. In fact, worse than that, we all have a theologian of glory living inside us. I know I do at times. Only a theologian of the cross can chase it out. Humble, courageous, fruit-bearing Great Commission spirituality demands a cross-centered, Bible-dominated, Christ-united vision of all things.

As mentioned earlier, weakness is not a virtue. Neither is brokenness. Humility is. And humility is what God is working in us through weakness and brokenness. But humility takes courage to persevere. We can either harden up or soften up in weakness and brokenness. It takes courage to remain steadfast in humility beneath God's severe providences. It takes courage to remain tenderhearted before God. We must learn to interpret our weaknesses as occasions of grace where we come to the end of ourselves and see God in Christ.

Consider the story of Jacob. He was a deceiver, through and through. He received the promise through faith, but he was going to do what was right in his own eyes. He came from a classic dysfunctional family. They put the "fun" in dysfunctional—everyone playing everyone else. As the consequences of a life of deceit came to a head, Jacob found himself wrestling with God (a pre-incarnate Christ) one night (Gen 32:22–30).

The Lord touched his hip and put it out of joint. In that struggle and striving, the Lord gave Jacob a new name: "Your name shall no longer be called Jacob, but Israel, for you have striven with God and with men, and have prevailed" (Gen 32:28). Israel means, "he strives with God." Then the Lord blessed him, and Jacob renamed that place "Peniel," which means, "I have seen God face to face" (Gen 32:30), or "facing God." He left the next morning, "limping because of his hip" (Gen 30:31).

There are layers of analogies (not allegories) to examine in this story. To be sure, this is part of a redemptive story greater than just Jacob's personal sanctification. This story is not a psychological commentary about our dysfunction. Yet in a way, it is instructive for us: "For whatever was written in former days was written for our instruction, that through endurance and through encouragement of the Scriptures we might have hope" (Rom 15:4).

Jacob's wrestling with God and consequent limp can be analogous of our lives in the Lord's service. Jacob was chosen to carry the Messiah Seed as part of the line of God's promise to bless the nations in Christ. Jacob knew it. He was determined to make it happen his way. But the promises are promises, not potentials. God will always make good on what he has promised. All of us have mixed motives, like Jacob's. We want to glorify God in the Great Commission, but we also want something else along with it—the praise of men, a sense of success, adventure, fun cultural experiences, a happy family, to prove ourselves as radical Christians. We can easily add our own secret ambitions to this list.

Inevitably, God wrestles us to the ground through some painful providences. We might have the stamina to struggle for a long night, so to speak. But eventually morning dawns and the Lord pulls back. There in that place of struggle, we realize we have seen God's face. It is like our Peniel. But we have only seen his face in the person of Christ Jesus. We were not consumed because Christ consumed the wrath of God for us. We could take the wounds of love because Christ took the wounds of judgment. God was rich in mercy toward us because he showed no mercy on the cross. As we share in the spiritual inheritance of spiritual Israel, we are among the many, like Israel, who "strive with God." Whether or not we are honest about it, we are all strugglers. And God has neither smote us nor let us go. We wrestle with omnipotence and are not obliterated. We wrestle with benevolence and receive a limp.

Because God is full of goodness toward us in Christ, he often sends us unique thorns in the flesh to keep us from becoming conceited. And that is indeed a temptation, especially for Great Commission servants. We can relish the rush of being on the frontlines of kingdom expansion and of receiving the adulation of supporting churches who praise us for our sacrifice. Conceit is deadly to the soul. God knows it, and he wrestles it out of our clutches. What is a sign that we have struggled with God and have seen his face in Christ? We walk with a metaphorical limp.

Paul pulls no punches in describing the gravity of this thorn: "a thorn was given me in the flesh, a messenger of Satan to harass me, to keep me from becoming conceited" (2 Cor 12:7). God sent Paul a thorn whose source was demonic for the purpose of keeping him humble. Paul, whose handkerchief touched people and healed them (Acts 19:12), prayed repeatedly for relief

(2 Cor 12:8). But God's reply was not what Paul expected. He replied with grace for courage and grace for power: "But he said to me, 'My grace is sufficient for you, for my power is made perfect in weakness.' Therefore I will boast all the more gladly of my weaknesses, so that the power of Christ may rest upon me" (2 Cor 12:9). Paul exuded humility and courage to embrace his limp. Paul rejoiced in the promise that Christ's power would rest upon him through his weakness. And that discovery of the power of Christ in him for service, in spite of his sufferings, led him to courageous contentment in Christ (2 Cor 12:9–10).

Paul's life is a picture of Great Commission spirituality resting in union with Christ, serving in obscurity and humility of heart. His courageous soul was marked by a glad-hearted contentment in God, come what may. All of Paul's inimitable virtues, from humility all the way to courage, grew out of his union with Christ. W. C. Burns said rightly about this union:

> UNION TO CHRIST! Here is the difference, here is the distinction, here is the life-giving principle, that has been inspired into the new created heart by the Holy Spirit. ... Union to Jesus is the humble Christian's life, his hope, his all, leave him but this, and you may take what you will away from him. It makes his trials, his afflictions, his losses, his sorrows, his griefs, not only supportable, not only endurable, but precious, sweet, a cause of thanksgiving, a matter for glory, just because in them—in the very severest, the very hottest—that union is always the more closely cemented.[9]

Courage and Self-Denial

In recent years, Bible colleges and seminaries in the West have been closing down their missions departments. Even the legacy institutions that served as flagship schools for missions and intercultural studies are shuttering these programs. Every case is different, of course. But the common reason is for lack of enrollment and funding. On the other hand, the departments that are growing the fastest in enrollment and financial incentives are the counseling departments. Isn't that fascinating? What does that say about the priorities of the emerging Christian generations? What does that say about evangelicalism's perceived needs?

---

9 Burns, *Notes of Address*, 198.

A combination of a few things could be true: Christians are increasingly aware of their need to work through the baggage in their lives; perhaps the ordinary means of grace found in receiving the word, prayer, the Lord's table, and loving fellowship feel like they are ineffective or impractical; perhaps the dire eternal needs of the unreached seem increasingly inconsequential or irrelevant to our lives; or maybe an introspective generation has emerged who believes their *telos* in life is to discover their broken places and find healing. Whatever the reasons are, the Lord knows.

God is not worried, however. Many of us love the quote from Esther 4:14 that says "And who knows whether you have not come to the kingdom for such a time as this?" But the first part of the verse is rarely quoted: "For if you keep silent at this time, relief and deliverance will rise for the Jews from another place, but you and your father's house will perish." In other words, God gives us opportunities in our vocations, nationalities, eras, and general life contexts to obey the Great Commission. He designs these according to the measure of grace, faith, and strength he has allotted each of us. But, if we hold back in fear or self-preservation, God will get the job done with someone else. It doesn't mean we are unsaved. It doesn't mean we mess up God's plans. And it doesn't mean he needs us one bit. It just means that we lose the privilege and the pleasure of abiding with Christ as he extends the reach of his global empire.

Sadly, too many potential Great Commission servants wait for the proverbial shiver in their liver, the most epic opportunity, innumerable confirmed signs, inner impressions of peace, and the most convenient task. Some expect a perfect open door that corresponds to their self-discovered passions, strengths, abilities, temperament, and personality profile. Yet, we are missing out on the joy, freedom, and privilege of self-forgetfulness. What better way to get outside ourselves and forget ourselves than to spend ourselves for the eternal good of the nations?

In Isaiah 58, God chastises Israel for its fake humility and empty-hearted rituals and fasts. They became so inward-focused that they neglected the needs of the impoverished around them. Instead of focusing on the usefulness of religious rituals and pious language, God calls them to spend themselves for the poor, the forgotten, the hungry, and the unreached (Isa 58:7, 9–10). The Lord says, "Then shall your light break forth like the dawn, and your healing shall spring up speedily; your righteousness shall go before you; the glory of the LORD shall be your rear guard" (Isa 58:8).

The theological context is different for us this side of the New Covenant. Christ fulfilled what Israel failed to do. The prophecy in Malachi mirrors what Isaiah is holding out here: "The sun of righteousness shall rise with healing in his wings. You shall go out leaping like calves from the stall" (Mal 4:2). This joy of healing, laughter, and light will be ours when we truly experience our union with the resurrected Christ at his return. We can take note of where we struggle, meditate on God's love for us, put our junk behind us, and spend our lives for the unreached. Jesus has secured and now safeguards our healing, righteousness, and honor. The joy of the Lord is our strength in Great Commission spirituality and service.

Here is a massively counter-cultural, unpopular opinion: self-denial is an abandoned feature of Great Commission service that separates the longsuffering servants of previous generations from a whole new generation of those who feel the need for counseling instead of missions. Self-denial in itself, however, is not technically a virtue. But it does fit under the categories of self-control/temperance, humility, and courage/fortitude. Biblical self-denial is not ascetic in the monastic, mystical sense. It doesn't seek to accrue merits or climb the ladder to union with Christ. Biblical self-denial for Great Commission spirituality rests in its union with Christ and makes choices that are potentially threatening or unsafe in love for the lost and forgotten.

Fundamentally, self-denial resting in union with Christ does not even view life as its own. Death is not a tragedy:

> For none of us lives to himself, and none of us dies to himself. For if we live, we live to the Lord, and if we die, we die to the Lord. So then, whether we live or whether we die, we are the Lord's. For to this end Christ died and lived again, that he might be Lord both of the dead and of the living. (Rom 14:7–9)

Biblical self-denial by faith acts upon the promises of God out of love for the lost. It walks by faith in such a way that can only be explained by a secure hope in the resurrected Christ and a future resurrection:

> These all died in faith, not having received the things promised, but having seen them and greeted them from afar, and having acknowledged that they were strangers and exiles on the earth. For people who speak thus make it clear that they are seeking a homeland. If they had been thinking of that land from which

> they had gone out, they would have had opportunity to return. But as it is, they desire a better country, that is, a heavenly one. Therefore God is not ashamed to be called their God, for he has prepared for them a city. (Heb 11:13–16)

Courage and the Constraining Love of Christ

We either love God above ourselves or love ourselves above God. The eighteenth and nineteenth century missionaries like Jonathan Edwards, Samuel Hopkins, David Brainerd, and Adoniram and Ann Judson upheld the necessity of self-denial and self-sacrifice in order to reach the unreached. They called it a "disinterested benevolence"—a love that is so captive to the glory of God and the good of the lost that it would give anything to see God glorified in the salvation of the nations. Such benevolence would suffer any loss to see the nations rejoice in the glory of God's grace.

Contrary to natural assumptions, balanced, Biblical self-denial should not give way to "self-murder"—a preventable early death, avoidable health problems, or suicide. Judson rejected the idea of self-made martyrdom or self-murder by ruining one's health to the point of an untimely death. But he also rejected the temptation to take a more comfortable post as a professor in America or a translator in a British colony. His courageous self-denial led him to endure in the task of translating the Bible, taking necessary precautions when sick. He never gave up, even if it meant getting deathly ill at times. In his last weeks of life, Judson's final sickness forced him out to sea in the hope that sea air would revive his health. He believed that if he stayed in Burma his sickness would kill him. He said to his wife with a courageous spirit of disinterested benevolence:

> Death will never take me by surprise—do not be afraid of that—I feel so strong in Christ. He has not led me so tenderly thus far to forsake me at the very gate of heaven. No, no; I am willing to live a few years longer if it should be so ordered; and if otherwise, I am willing and glad to die now. I leave myself entirely in the hands of God, to be disposed of according to his holy will.[10]

Five years before Judson's death at sea, he spoke to a group of would-be missionaries at his *alma mater*, Brown University. Here is how Judson's

10 Burns, *Supreme Desire to Please*, 109.

long life of abiding in Christ's love influenced him to think of Great Commission spirituality. He spoke of the loving duty that propels self-sacrifice to courageously endure to the end:

> Judson began a long conclusion by warning not to follow enthusiasm, impressions, and emotions, for Satan often counterfeits truth with such feelings. However, he instructed them to seek to follow "a deep and abiding conviction of duty" that essentially cries, "Woe is me if I preach not the Gospel to the heathen." Judson said this sense of duty alone would "sustain a man under the severe trials and labors of the missionary life," and no man would stay the course without such a settled conviction of duty that is "constrained by the love of Christ," in order to "lead many more, to love him." He concluded by saying, "But with the assurance that, having humbly submitted himself to the Divine teaching, he has the approval of Christ, he is prepared for any event. With this he can labor; by this he can die. If brought into difficulties, from which there seems no escape, he feels that he has gone thus far in obedience to his Lord's command; that he is doing his Master's work; and that, whatever befalls him, all is well: it is the will of Christ."[11]

A year later, in an address to the Foreign Mission Board of the Southern Baptist Convention, Judson divulged the secret to courage in a life of self-denial and self-sacrifice in Christ's service. He asked, "What, then, is the prominent, all-constraining impulse that should urge us to make sacrifices in this cause?" And he answered his own question by highlighting the excellence of Christ's union with humanity and how he "at a great expense" to himself gave up himself lovingly to establish sinners into his good kingdom. In view of such a benevolent King and a marvelous kingdom, Judson made his case: "A supreme desire to please him is the grand motive that should animate Christians in their missionary efforts."[12]

God providentially designed Judson's courage to deny himself the pleasures of life in America and easier ministry positions. Interestingly, among the Burmese Buddhists, the holy men sought self-denial for the sake of meriting good karma and eventually nirvana. The monks denied

11 Burns, 122.

12 Burns, 180.

themselves basic pleasures because desire is the root cause of bad karma. The Burmese thought they knew what self-denial looked like until Judson, his family, and missionary team arrived. They observed Judson's courage to lose wives and children to their climate and diseases and still remain serving among them. They observed Judson's courage to spend his whole adult life, day after day, for the translation of a sacred text into their native language. All this labor for which he would never receive payment or reward.

Even further, they observed Judson suffer unremitting torture for almost two years in a Burmese prison for the false accusation that he was a British spy. And upon release, instead of abandoning the Burmese for their shameful treatment of him, he showed them the honor of staying among them and getting back to work on the sacred text. They watched him whittle his life down through years of sickness, sadness, depression, and eventually the loss of his own voice due to an infection. He did this voluntarily only for the sake of loving Christ and the Burmese people. When he was sick, at the end of his life, he went to sea (not back to America) with the hope of returning to finish the dictionary.

Judson's life of disinterested benevolence for the salvation of the Burmese Buddhists communicated an otherworldly self-denial that they had never before witnessed in their Buddhist monks. The so-called "holy" monks denied their personal desires. But they recognized that Judson's supernatural courage and humility were rooted in a good, holy desire to honor Christ and give them the Scripture through self-sacrifice. That sacred book became known as "the golden lamp hung out of heaven to enlighten the nations that sit in darkness."[13] Knowing that the love of Christ constrained him, Buddhists and animists would come from all around, even from the nations bordering the Burmese empire, to inquire: "Are you Jesus Christ's man? Give us a writing that tells us about Jesus Christ."[14]

Courage to Finish Well

Many courageous saints of old have stood alone, against all odds, in the darkest hour. In the heat of battle, they thanked God for his presence and took courage: Noah spent decades building an ark in the desert where

13 Burns, 78.

14 Burns, 4.

it had never rained, bearing the mocking and abuse of the locals. Moses stood in the courts of Pharaoh, threatening the most powerful man in the world with plagues on behalf of God and his people. Samson, after a deeply flawed life lived by faith, leaned blindly on the pillars of the Philistine temple. With one last judgment, he took down all the Philistines along with himself in hope that God would save his soul according to his promises.

In the presence of the cowardly Israelite army, David charged a giant with only a sling and a stone. Elijah mocked the prophets of Baal and called upon God to rain fire out of heaven. Daniel showed no compromise in his prayers to God and was thrown to the lions. Shadrach, Meshach, and Abednego refused to forsake the God of Israel and walked to the fiery furnace. Esther approached the king, though it was against the law, and said, "If I perish, I perish."

John the Baptist lost his head for condemning the sexual immorality of Herod's family. Stephen looked to the ascendant Christ as the stones were flying at his face. Paul, standing before magistrates, governors, and religious leaders, never stopped speaking boldly of the risen King. God gave some the grace of deliverance. Others, he gave the grace of martyrdom. Some were handled with tenderness, others handed over to torture. But as Paul would say in his final letter, amidst all the slander, abandonment, and torture, Jesus was with him. Jesus was also with his saints in the fiery furnace, the lion's den, the exodus, and every other deliverance in the Bible. W. C. Burns well said,

> When that cry ascends, an answer comes; and, ah, then there is a bond formed, which neither time, nor death, nor hell, can ever rend: and when He ties the eternal knot, believe it, nor death nor hell can break it. "Who shall separate us from the love of Christ?" … Will not the Lord save and guard His own truth? The saints may be imprisoned, ministers silenced or banished, God's people may be *hung up* for the truth's sake, but the truth itself will not be hung up or stifled. No, it will spread, it will run, it will be glorified in times like these. The truth of Christ, and the saints' union to Him, will … spring up into beauty and renown from their open graves.[15]

Paul mused on the Lord's abiding presence in those moments: "But the Lord stood by me and strengthened me" (2 Tim 4:17). To what end

15 Burns, *Notes of Address*, 109–10. Emphasis in original.

does Christ stand by us? Paul says it in the next clause: "so that through me the message might be fully proclaimed and all the Gentiles might hear it." Christ abides with us for the sake of his gospel and the good of the nations.

Many kings in the Old Testament started off well in their service to God but finished poorly. Cowardice diminished their courage. Very few finished well. Even today, very few seem to run their race well to the finish line. This does not always mean they prove to be unsaved. Most are just strugglers and their secret sins come to light after years of being afraid to honestly address them. Truth and time eventually meet.

Let us not be so preoccupied with building our resume that we forget we are dealing with souls not projects. Let us remember someone will prepare our eulogy someday and etch something brief on our gravestone indicative of the legacy they perceive that we left. Let us have the courage to keep the word of Christ with the power he supplies. Let us leave a legacy of fruitfulness that lasts for eternity.

Prayerful Instinct to Abide in Christ with Courage

Courage to trust in Christ, to love faithfully, and to live by hope in God's ancient promises is the pattern of Great Commission spirituality. Courage to do this in Great Commission service comes from an abiding prayerful instinct in union with Christ that meditates on the word. It contemplates God's good creation. It witnesses to Christ's gospel. And it walks with God and before others in humility. Let us pray without ceasing, not because we fear everything, but because Christ is in us and with us and for us in everything. He is our victory.

When we are at the end of our reserves and feel like we cannot get out of bed, when we cannot live another day, when we wake up surprised that we are still breathing and not dead, what then? Let us remember Jesus. Abide in him with a prayerful instinct. The life of Christ works in us courage to press on to do what we must do.

After the death of a spouse or a child, as we sit down to write their obituary, wrapping up all the details of bereavement, God gives us the courage to keep proclaiming his love in Christ. To those watching, we might seem broken and in need of healing. To Christ, we are his and in need of him. He is enough now in bereavement just as much as he was in abundance. He who has Christ and all the world has no more than he who has Christ alone. The battered, bleeding heart limps through this life with waves of regrets, griefs, nightmares, sad memories, and bad memories. Yet it can look to Christ with the boldness of a lion: "Whom have I in heaven but you? And there is nothing on earth that I desire besides you. My flesh and my heart may fail, but God is the strength of my heart and my portion forever" (Ps 73:25–26).

> *It is emphatically no sacrifice. Say rather it is a privilege. Anxiety, sickness, suffering, or danger, now and then, with a foregoing of the common conveniences and charities of this life, may make us pause, and cause the spirit to waver, and the soul to sink; but let this only be for a moment. All these are nothing when compared with the glory which shall be revealed in and for us. I never made a sacrifice.*
>
> —David Livingstone

Conclusion

One with Christ in Life and in Death

Scripture for Meditation

For me to live is Christ, and to die is gain.

—Philippians 1:21

Simon of Cyrene was minding his own business in Jerusalem one day as he was trying to make his way through a riotous crowd. He then saw a criminal stumble under the weight of a Roman cross. Blood and mud splattered on Simon's sandal. In a seemingly random flurry of events, a soldier snagged Simon's cloak. He ordered that Simon relieve the prisoner of his rugged cross.

The criminal was repulsive with his flayed, swollen flesh, blood, and vomit. But as Simon shouldered the cross to carry it, something drew him to the man. It wasn't so much that he himself had compassion for the prisoner as much as he perceived the man genuinely had compassion for him. In fact, as the criminal limped next to him, something of the man gave Simon the strength he needed to haul the wooden beams up to Golgotha.

Simon couldn't exactly understand why this criminal was guilty, but the people kept demanding he be crucified for claiming to be the Son of God. Whatever the case, this man was no common criminal or ordinary religious leader. He muttered over and over with blood in his mouth, "Sacrifices and offerings you have not desired, but a body have you prepared for me" (Heb 10:5). Simon made it to the top of the hill and slowly walked away after being discharged of his duty. He mingled amongst the onlookers who were apparently the criminal's friends. What they told him arrested his conscience as he walked all the way back home.

Stumbling through the door of his home, his wife and son greeted him with their lips curled and their noses snarled. Dad looked even worse than he smelled. "What is that blood all over you?" they clamored in fear. He explained that it was not his own, just the marks from a bloody cross. He explained that he was ordered to carry a criminal's cross as though it were his own. The criminal walked with him and talked to him on the way. But at the place of death, the man took his place on the cross and was executed.

Simon paused and said, "But I walked away free. In fact, I believe he was the Son of God. He seemed to give me the strength to carry the cross. Though I stood by him, truly I saw that it was he who stood by me. In my place condemned he stood." Years later, Simon's wife would minister to the Apostle Paul's needs, and Rufus, Simon's son, would become a missionary (Rom 16:13), taking the message of the criminal's cross to the nations. He would imitate the faith of his father, proclaiming as it were: "He bore the shame and scoffing rude, and in my place condemned he stood. Hallelujah, What a Savior!"[1]

One with Our Savior-King

Consider the above illustration as a simple analogy of Great Commission spirituality. A life devoted to Christ in Great Commission service can feel cruciform—bearing on our body the marks of Jesus. Those marks might look like a hardened face, with both smile lines and a furrowed brow. It might be chronic headaches and indigestion. It could be depleted strength from viruses, fevers, vaccines, and malnutrition. It might be shaky hands from beatings to the head and spine, or a broken heart that leaves you daily on the brink of tears. Maybe it's tormenting thoughts of suicide. Maybe it's demonic dreams.

1 *Hymns of Grace*, "Hallelujah, What a Savior!" #296.

Great Commission spirituality calls those in Christ's service like the mountains call the mountain men. It is a sacred place that can evoke fear at times. But every day in the haunts of the wilderness is like a dream come true. It is the hardest and the happiest life. It is the arena where our mettle is tested, again and again. Christ calls those serving actively in the Great Commission to a life of obscurity and ordinary obedience. It is a summons to a long life of labor and self-denial. It is an invitation to a prayerful instinct of communion with Christ.

Christ's servants draw from his power to preach the gospel in season and out of season. But this is no terrifying assignment. Indeed, it is an extraordinary privilege to lose everything to gain a sweeter, more excellent fellowship with him. Through tears, torrents, and the torture of the soul, Christ is there, with us, in us, over us, and before us. He is enough, truly, more than enough.

As William Carey famously remarked about Christ's abiding presence, "All my friends are but one … I rejoice that he is all sufficient and can supply all my wants, spiritual and temporal."[2] His grace is sufficient for his tasks. John G. Paton reflected on the sweetness of our union with Christ and prayerfully abiding in his presence:

> Our safety lay in our appeal to that blessed Lord who had placed us there, and to whom all power had been given in Heaven and on Earth. He that was with us was more than all that could be against us. This is strength; this is peace—to feel, in entering on every day, that all its duties and trials have been committed to the Lord Jesus,—that, come what may, He will use us for His own glory and our real good. All through that dreadful morning, and far into the afternoon, we thus abode together, feeling conscious that we were united to this dear Lord Jesus, and we had sweet communion with Him, meditating on the wonders of His person and the hopes and glories of His kingdom. Oh, that all my readers may learn something of this in their own experience of the Lord. I can wish them nothing more precious.[3]

Jesus's grace and goodness make up for the losses, even deep losses. Let the light of our union with Christ shine through the windows of his

2 Carey, *Journal*, 33.

3 Paton, *John G. Paton*, 2456.

word and his world to refresh us. Let us always look to him for the smiling face of God. God has united us to Christ in love that neither improves nor diminishes based upon our performance. Great Commission spirituality prayerfully abides in Christ, filled with the word of Christ, suffers with Christ, proclaims Christ, and gains Christ:

> But whatever gain I had, I counted as loss for the sake of Christ. Indeed, I count everything as loss because of the surpassing worth of knowing Christ Jesus my Lord. For his sake I have suffered the loss of all things and count them as rubbish, in order that I may gain Christ and be found in him, not having a righteousness of my own that comes from the law, but that which comes through faith in Christ, the righteousness from God that depends on faith—that I may know him and the power of his resurrection, and may share his sufferings, becoming like him in his death, that by any means possible I may attain the resurrection from the dead. (Phil 3:7–11)

May we spend ourselves in union with Christ for the good of the unreached and the glory of God. We will be among those nameless, faceless saints in the end who have conquered the devil "by the blood of the Lamb and by the word of their testimony, for they loved not their lives even unto death" (Rev 21:11). Let us be counted as those "who follow the Lamb wherever he goes" (Rev 14:4), whose tattered banner declares: "Your steadfast love is better than life" (Ps 63:3).

> *Brethren, look to Jesus. This sight will fill you with the greatest consolation and delight. Look to Him on the cross; so great is His love that, if He had a thousand lives, He would lay them all down for your redemption. Look to Him on the throne; His blessed countenance fills all heaven with delight and felicity. Look to Him in affliction; He will succor you. Look to Him in death; He will sustain you. Look to Him in the judgment; He will save you.*
>
> —Adoniram Judson

Acknowledgments

No one is an island, and no book is entirely from one's own innovation. We are all the products of our education, our relationships, and our experiences. God uses his people and his providences to form us into Christ's image in unique ways. The pages of this book derive from years of teaching these topics in seminaries and other ministries around the world. Yet, I will be the first to admit that I rarely have an original idea. The content of my lectures, sermons, and books come from decades of study under great men of God whom I hope to imitate as they imitate Christ.

I wish to acknowledge some of those brothers who have influenced the spirit and content of this book through both formal instruction and informal discipleship. I could spend a whole page listing them all, but these men in particular were spiritual mentors whose insights reminded me to abide in the word of Christ and so formed what and how I teach: Bill Thrasher, Dave Wickstrom, Rod Rosenbladt, Michael Haykin, Don Whitney, Mike Abendroth, Rick Holland, Jerry Root, Lyle Dorsett, Gerry Breshears, John Gates, Tom Ascol, Andy Hamilton, and my father, Dan Burns.

I wish to thank those brothers who encourage my writing and give me strong feedback and helpful advice: Ben Mosier, Garret Nelson, Joe Goeman, Nate Carson, Ben Orchard, Chris Martin, Caleb Klontz, Joe Fauth, Joseph White, Aaron Cunningham, Kyle Schwahn, Darren Carlson, Ken Brown, Luke Lacey, Dustin Benge, Brian Fairchild, Chad Vegas, Alex Kocman, Jim Osman, Blake Valley, Matt Jensen, Jared Hla, John Htaw, John Leaf, Kyle Davis, Steve Meister, Chris Burnett, Mark Tatlock, Eric Weathers, Peter Sammons, Trent Hunter, Karl Dahlfred, Dan Baber, Derek Joseph, Neel Roberts, Pete Sharp, Mike Sidders, Tim Bohrer, Matthew Villandry, John Vance, Andrew Goodman, Scott Callaham, Anthony Barton, Jason Butler, Matt Glass, Bill Sanders, Alex White, Scotty Wharton, Steve Allen, Lloyd Abiva, Eugene Low, Billy Coppedge, Tanner Heath, Barry King, and Stephen Langley. I am also very grateful to both Matt Bennett and John Tucker for reading most of my first draft manuscripts and giving me constructive feedback. And I'm grateful to Karen Hedinger for helping me format the final manuscript.

I wish to thank my family for their undying support year after year: Mike, Mindy, Emily, Dale, Debbie, Allison, Bethany, Lindsey, Claire,

Gracie, Sandra, and mom and dad. I cannot imagine who I would be (and who I would not be) without your love, support, and esteem. Thank you for standing by me. I am speechless as I think of how kind God has been to entrust me with Elijah and Isaiah. Your unbreakable spirit and admiration encourage me to be faithful in the duties God has given us. And most of all, the Lord has been immeasurably gracious in giving me Dao. Your daily affection and respect fill me with joy and strength to persevere in Great Commission service. You are a gift from God. I love you forever.

Look past me and see Jesus. He is your life. He is your hope. He is your all.

E. D. BURNS
Southeast Asia

Bibliography

Augustine. *City of God*. New York: Penguin Books, 2004.

Augustine. *Confessions*. New York: Penguin Books, 1961.

Bainton, Roland Herbert. *Here I Stand: A Life of Martin Luther*. Peabody, MA: Hendrickson Publishers, 1950.

Berry, Wendell. *The Unsettling of America*. Berkley, CA: Counterpoint Press, 2015.

Burns, E. D. *Ancient Gospel, Brave New World: Jesus Still Saves Sinners in Cultures of Shame, Fear, Bondage, and Weakness*. Cape Coral, FL: Founders Press, 2021.

Burns, E. D. "A Case for the Missionary as Preacher." *Pro Pastor: A Journal of Grace Bible Theological Seminary* 2, no. 1 (Spring 2023): 18–25.

Burns, E. D. *Karmic Christianity: Finding Peace by Faith Alone*. Littleton, CO: William Carey Publishing, 2023.

Burns, E. D. *The Missionary-Theologian: Sent into the World, Sanctified by the Word*. Ross-shire, UK: Christian Focus, 2020.

Burns, E. D. *Seeds and Stars: Resting in Christ for Great Commission Service*. Cape Coral, FL: Founders, 2023.

Burns, E. D. *A Supreme Desire to Please Him: The Spirituality of Adoniram Judson*. Eugene, OR: Pickwick Publications, 2016.

Burns, E. D. *The Transcultural Gospel: Jesus Is Enough for Sinners in Cultures of Shame, Fear, Bondage, and Weakness*. Cape Coral, FL: Founders Press, 2021.

Burns, Islay. *Memoir of William C. Burns, Missionary to China*. San Francisco: Chinese Materials Center, 1975.

Burns, W. C. *Notes of Addresses*. London: James Nisbet, 1869.

Burns, W. C. *Revival Sermons*. Edinburgh: Banner of Truth, 1981.

Calvin, John. *Institutes of the Christian Religion*. The Library of Christian Classics. Vol. 1. Edited by John T. McNeill. Translated by Ford Lewis Battles. Louisville, KY: Westminster John Knox Press, 2006.

Carey, William. *The Journal and Selected Letters of William Carey*. Edited by Terry G. Carter. Macon, GA: Smyth & Helwys Publishing, 2022.

Dante. *Paradiso: A Verse Translation by Robert Hollander and Jean Hollander*. New York: Anchor Books, 2007.

Dorsett, Lyle W. *Seeking the Secret Place: The Spiritual Formation of C. S. Lewis*. Grand Rapids, MI: Brazos Press, 2004.

Edwards, Jonathan. *The Works of Jonathan Edwards*. Vol. I & II. Revised by Edward Hickman. Edinburgh: Banner of Truth Trust, 1974. Kindle.

Elliot, Elisabeth. *Keep a Quiet Heart*. Grand Rapids, MI: Revell, 1995.

Flavel, John. *Major Works of John Flavel*. N.p. Midas Classics, 2016. Kindle Edition.

Grosart, Alexander Balloch. *The Complete Works of Richard Sibbes*. Vol. 7. Edinburgh: J. Nichol, 1864. Kindle.

Holden, J. Stuart. "Foreword." In J. Hudson Taylor, *Union and Communion (1893), or Thoughts on the Song of Solomon*. 3rd ed. *The Hudson Taylor 7-in-1 Collection*. Christian Classics Treasury, 2012. Kindle Edition.

Houghton, S. M. *Five Pioneer Missionaries: David Brainerd, William C. Burns, John Eliot, Henry Martyn, John G. Paton*. Edinburgh: Banner of Truth Trust, 1987.

Hymns of Grace. "Hallelujah, What a Savior!" #296. Los Angeles: The Master's Seminary Press, 2015.

Jacobs, Alan. *The Narnian: The Life and Imagination of C. S. Lewis*. New York: HarperCollins, 2009. Kindle Edition.

Lewis, C. S. *Mere Christianity*. New York: HarperCollins, 1980.

Lewis, C. S. *The Screwtape Letters*. New York: HarperCollins, 1996.

Luther, Martin. *Career of the Reformer I*. American Edition. Edited by Jaroslav Pelikan and Helmut T. Lehmann. Vol. 31 of Luther's Works. Edited by Harold J. Grimm. Philadelphia: Muhlenberg and Fortress, 1957.

Luther, Martin. *Sermons 1*. Edited by Helmut T. Lehmann and John W. Doberstein. Vol. 51 of Luther's Works. Philadelphia: Fortress Press, 1959.

McMullen, Michael D. *God's Polished Arrow: Wiliam Chalmers Burns*. Ross-shire, UK: Christian Focus, 2000.

Mounce, William D. *Mounce's Complete Expository Dictionary of Old and New Testament Words*. Grand Rapids, MI: Zondervan Academic, 2006.

Murray, John. *Collected Writings of John Murray: Life; Sermons; Reviews*. Vol. 3. Edinburgh: Banner of Truth Publishing, 1991.

Navigators. "The Word Hand Illustration." Accessed November 1, 2023. https://www.navigators.org/resource/the-word-hand/.

Paton, John G. *John G. Paton: Missionary to the New Hebrides, An Autobiography*. Miami: HardPress, 2017. Kindle.

Rigney, Joe. *Lewis on the Christian Life: Becoming Truly Human in the Presence of God*. Wheaton, IL: Crossway, 2018.

Root, Jerry, and Stan Guthrie. *The Sacrament of Evangelism*. Chicago: Moody Publishers, 2011.

Spurgeon, Charles. *Morning and Evening*. Grand Rapids, MI: Discovery House, 2016.

Taylor, Dr. Howard, and Mrs. Howard Taylor. *Hudson Taylor's Spiritual Secret*. Chicago: Moody Publishers, 2009.

Taylor, Hudson. *The Hudson Taylor Collection, 7-in-1: A Retrospect, Union and Communion, Separation and Service, Ribband of Blue, Taylor in Early Years, Growth of a Work of God, Choice Sayings*. Christian Classics Treasury, 2012.

Taylor, Hudson. *Union and Communion: Reflections on the Song of Solomon*. Apollo, PA: Icthus Publishing, 2017.

Taylor, Justin. "How Much Do You Have to Hate Somebody *Not* to Proselytize?" *The Gospel Coalition*. November 18, 2009. https://www.thegospelcoalition.org/blogs/justin-taylor/how-much-do-you-have-to-hate-somebody-to-not-proselytize/.

The Three Forms of Unity. The Reformed Church of the United States, 2011. Kindle.

Watson, Thomas. "How We May Read the Scriptures with Most Spiritual Profit." In *Puritan Sermons*. Vol. 2, 1674. Reprint Wheaton, IL: Richard Owen Roberts, 1981.

Watson, Thomas. *The Works of Thomas Watson: Containing Seven of Watson's Best Loved Works*. Ted Cortez Publishing, 2018. Kindle Edition.

Whitney, Donald S. *Spiritual Disciplines for the Christian Life*. Colorado Springs: Navpress, 1991.

Wirt, Sherwood Eliot, ed. *Spiritual Disciplines: Devotional Writings from the Great Christian Leaders of the Seventeenth Century*. Wheaton, IL: Crossway, 1983.

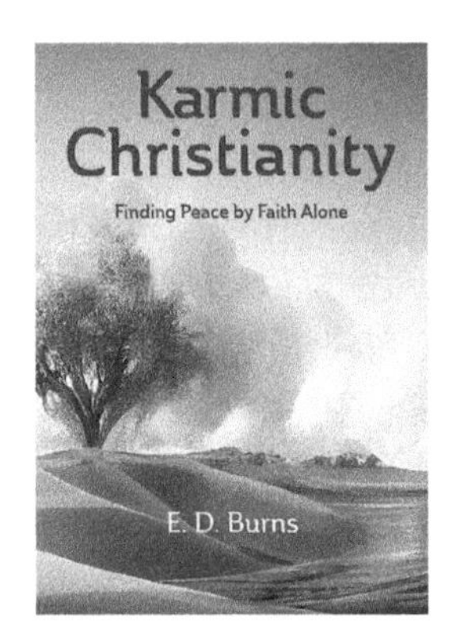

Karmic Christianity:
Finding Peace by Faith Alone
E. D. Burns

We can too easily fall into a karmic-like cycle of good works, relying on our own power to break the cycle of fear. E. D. Burns explains why the antidote to fear is not power but rather peace—God's peace. The peace of Christ sets us free from anxiety arising from hardships and our inability to control our situations. Burns shows why the solution is not working harder, being better, or just giving up. Readers learn why we don't need to be exhausted. Instead, we can rest in God's refuge, trusting that his love for us is perfect in Christ.

Spirituality in Mission:
Embracing the Lifelong Journey

John Amalraj, Geoffrey W. Hahn, William D. Taylor, editors

Authors from eighteen countries give us their perspectives on biblical principles and cultural expressions of spirituality, particularly as the church engages in God's mission. The issue today is how spirituality should direct and guide daily life as followers of Jesus in the engagement in the mission of God. This book will help you rethink your understanding of what is spiritual, revisit your own spiritual journey, and appreciate the different forms of spirituality.

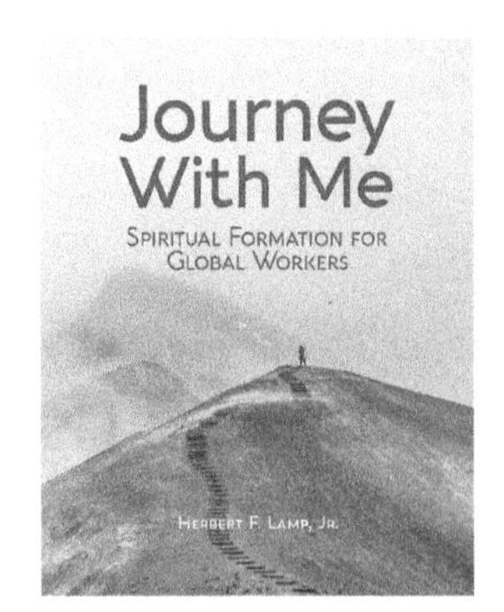

Journey With Me:
Spiritual Formation for Global Workers
Herbert F. Lamp, Jr.

Journey With Me illustrates that ministry is the result of the overflow of our relationship with God, rather than vice versa. Exploring over fifteen ancient spiritual graces—such as Lectio Divina, rule of life, silence and solitude, and prayer of Examen—Herbert F. Lamp, Jr. invites us to prioritize soul care, rather than treating ministry as a replacement for intimacy. In the process of knowing and being known, God fills us up with his love, joy, peace, and wisdom. Only then can we minister to others, balancing a heart for God with hands for service.